The Museum of Primitive Art • *Lecture Series Number Two*
THREE REGIONS OF PRIMITIVE ART

THREE REGIONS

Distributed by University Publishers, Inc. 1961

OF PRIMITIVE ART

Hallam L. Movius, Jr. • S. Kooijman • George Kubler
THE MUSEUM OF PRIMITIVE ART, NEW YORK

Distributed by University Publishers, Inc.
Copyright 1961, The Museum of Primitive Art
Printed in the United States of America by Davis, Delaney, Inc.
Typography by Bob Melson
Library of Congress Catalogue Card Number: 61-12117

CONTENTS

Robert Goldwater
FOREWORD

The three lectures that comprise this book are loosely joined by a single concern: each discusses in detail some one area of the broad and inclusive field which has come to be called primitive art. The authors treat their special subjects very differently.

Dr. Kooijman deals with a circumscribed area, the art of a still existing people whose description lies within the disciplines of ethnology. It is an art which, though recent, is yet entirely of the past, since the cultural conditions from which it sprang have been destroyed by the rapid impact of alien beliefs and techniques. From what we know of it, we conclude that its history was short, its geographical distribution extraordinarily restricted. Despite—or because of—these circumstances, there were evolved distinctive and unified styles, which produced works whose average quality was extremely high and included sculptures which we judge as masterpieces. Behind Dr. Kooijman's careful account lies the persistent question, how and why were the small groups of people living in western New Guinea able to create such art.

Dr. Movius, on the contrary, discusses an art of the long distant past, known to us only through archaeology. By an examination of exact detail, he wishes to clarify both the extent and the limitations of our knowledge, avoiding facile generalizations and conclusions reached by analogy with the art of other, more recent and very different, "primitive" peoples. The closeness of his argument around the finds of one particular site suggests the extent and complication of the whole field of pre-historic art, and the difficulties encountered in its interpretation. We are warned of the dangers of speculation, and made aware of the need for precision. Dr. Movius describes himself as a scientist and is skeptical of any but minimal conclusions about the artistic nature of these artifacts.

Dr. Kubler's argument is of a more theoretical kind. He, too, has only archaeological evidence on which to build—the remains of the material culture of pre-Columbian America — and he would call our attention to limitations, but of a very different sort. Contrasting the points of view of archaeologist and art historian, he suggests that the latter (a late-comer to the study of primitive art) can use his special, visually trained understanding of skills and styles to develop historical sequences that escape traditional procedures. More important, Dr. Kubler believes that, by the analysis of style as a fundamental fact, the art historian can help us understand some otherwise neglected qualities in the nature of a culture.

Each of these three lectures, the second series published by The Museum of Primitive Art, is concerned with a thorough investigation of one topic. Together, they point up the historical and theoretical breadth and depth of a varied area of the arts of man.

Hallam L. Movius, Jr.
ASPECTS OF UPPER PALAEOLITHIC ART

It is generally known that many fine examples of the art of Palaeolithic, or Old Stone Age, times occur in the depths of the natural limestone caves of southern France and northern Spain. At these localities representations of animals, including certain now-extinct types, have been discovered which are the artistic creations of various prehistoric groups of hunting peoples who lived some 10,000 to 30,000 years ago. This art is often referred to as "Cave Man's Art" or "Cro-Magnon Art," although there are only two known instances which suggest that Cro-Magnon Man was actually responsible for the drawings in question. Furthermore, the caves themselves were not occupied: prehistoric man normally chose for his camp-site either the terrace platform in front of the cave or the shelter under an overhanging rock, called *abri* in French.

No art exists as an abstraction apart from the cultural milieu in which it was produced. In other words, every artistic expression reflects the culture of the people who created it — the economic basis of their subsistence, their social organization, their ceremonial life. Since more than one Upper Palaeolithic culture is found in southern and western Europe which produced individuals with considerable artistic ability, more than one style of art was developed in this region during Old Stone Age times.

The fact that a number of distinct styles of artistic expression can be distinguished is not generally appreciated. Actually these can be grouped into two main cycles named after the cultures with which they are associated: (1) the Aurignacian-Périgordian cycle, and (2) the Magdalenian. But let us consider where these developments fall on the time-scale of man's prehistoric cultural development.

Palaeolithic archaeology deals with an almost incomprehensible span of time between the first appearance of man as an erect-walking, tool-using mammal and the beginnings of any written record — an interval of perhaps some million years' duration. For all but one-fiftieth of this period man was at the Palaeolithic, or Old Stone Age, level of cultural development. From the point of view of the geologic time-scale this covers the entire Pleistocene, or Glacial, Epoch, when the northern regions and mountainous areas of the globe were subjected to four successive advances and retreats of the ice-sheets (known in the Alps as Günz, Mindel, Riss and Würm), river valleys and terraces were being formed, and profound changes were being induced in the fauna and flora of the Earth. These major events were separated by intervals, known as interglacials, when climatic conditions prevailed which were even warmer than those of the present.

Throughout the entire span of the Palaeolithic Period man was a food-gatherer depending for his subsistence on hunting wild animals and birds, fishing, and collecting wild fruits, nuts and berries. The present evidence demonstrates that *three* main traditions were developed for the manufacture of stone implements. These are as follows: (1) core-tool traditions; (2) flake-tool traditions; and (3) blade-tool traditions. Various types of the last named characterize all the Upper Palaeolithic cultures of southern and western Europe, and it is with the several subdivisions of these cultures, the Aurignacian, Périgordian, Solutrean and Magdalenian, that we are concerned. There is no permanent evidence left whatsoever to suggest that art is older than the Aurignacian which began some 30,000 years ago, in western Europe.

Five main categories of artistic expression are known: (1) finger tracings, or "macaroni," in mud on the cave walls; (2) engravings; (3) bas-reliefs; (4) sculptures; and (5) paintings. In addition to representations on the walls of caves, very fine examples of art occur on fragments of bone, ivory, stone slabs, and water-worn pebbles. To this latter series, known as *art mobilier,* or portable art, belongs a group of figures in the round — small statuettes mostly of females which are some-

13

times found in association with Upper Périgordian occupation layers, although a few Aurignacian examples are known.

The data concerning the technique employed in producing figures in bas-relief on cave walls and large blocks of limestone are very meager. Presumably the limestone was chipped away with a chisel or pick of flint held in one hand and hit with a stone hammer wielded in the other, but this has never been definitely confirmed. More, however, is known concerning the engraved drawings. Both in the case of the cave wall art and the portable art objects, these were unquestionably produced by using burins or gravers of flint, which are found in great quantities in the occupation layers and deposits of the same localities where engravings have been discovered. In fact in a cave in the Pyreneean region of southern France, one of these tools was found actually resting on a small projecting knob of wall just below a very fine engraving of a cave lion.

Now the study of Upper Palaeolithic art can be approached from two entirely different points of view: (1) *stratigraphic* or *chronologic* — an objective approach, the aim of which is to provide the dating evidence necessary to serve as the basis for establishing an historical sequence or frame of reference for the various developmental stages, each with its distinctive style or combination of styles, that have been preserved for us; and (2) *aesthetic* — or the appreciation of this art for art's sake, so to speak. This is a completely subjective approach that, in many instances, is based more on romance and imagination than it is on fact. Somewhere between these two extremes lies another field that has to do with man's behavior as a social being. Necessarily speculative to some degree, it has a foundation on a large body of cumulative data, both prehistoric and contemporary or ethnographic. This third field of interpretation lies in the realm of the (3) *significance* of Upper Palaeolithic art. To explore this approach it is patently obvious that the documents in any given instance, whether paintings, engrav-

14

ings or sculptures, must be deciphered. To allude to them as "probably for ceremonial purposes" may appear plausible at first glance, but actually begs the issue and contributes nothing material and germane to our understanding of the purpose behind the artistic accomplishment. Finally, those interested in reconstructing the life and times of our prehistoric forerunners as fully as possible can utilize the information of what the (4) *now-extinct animals* depicted in the art looked like. In that a very remarkable degree of realism is the rule, this approach may be considered objective within certain limits.

The La Colombière Pebble
Evidence that has an interesting and direct bearing on each of these concepts or facets of Upper Palaeolithic art was brought to light in 1948 by the Peabody Museum of Harvard University's Expedition to eastern France sent out to excavate the Upper Palaeolithic rock-shelter of La Colombière, near Poncin (Ain). This site (plate 1) lies in the limestone uplands of the Lower Ain Valley, some 45 miles northeast of Lyons. Just prior to the outbreak of World War I it was partially excavated by Dr. Lucien Mayet and M. Jean Pissot with very significant results: the existence was established of an Upper Périgordian occupation layer at La Colombière containing not only a rich industry, but also a series of very interesting water-worn pebbles and large flat bones engraved in the best tradition of Old Stone Age art. This Upper Périgordian horizon was: (a) separated from the overlying Magdalenian III level by a one meter thick deposit of sterile sand, and (b) intercalated with the upper levels of a series of fluviatile silts, sands and gravels that constitute part of the twenty- to twenty-three-meter terrace of the Ain. This latter feature, which fills up the La Colombière rock-shelter to a depth of some twelve meters, has a very wide distribution in this region.

The stratigraphic evidence secured in 1948 shows that, as the period of formation of the twenty- to twenty-three-meter terrace of the Ain was drawing to a close, Upper Périgordian hunters moved into this section of the Ain Valley, presumably during the warm months of the year, and established a temporary camp on the valley floor, which at this time formed the base of the rock-shelter. Actually they were living on the surface of the then-existing fluvio-glacial flood plain of the Ain River at a point where this feature was protected by the overhanging rock now known as La Colombière.

A careful study of the archaeological material from this valuable site has demonstrated that the earliest occupation levels at this locality date from Upper Périgordian times. In view of the artistic attainments of these hunting peoples, their cultural affinities are especially important. In 1948, in association with a large hearth, in the east-central portion of the site, the Harvard Expedition discovered a very beautifully engraved pebble of fine-grained porcellaneous limestone 12 cm. long by 8.2 cm. wide and 3.5 cm. thick. Unfortunately it had been twice broken at one end, in antiquity.

plate 2   This object (plate 2) certainly testifies to the high artistic attainments and technical ability of certain individual member(s) of the group of Upper Périgordian hunters who settled at La Colombière. As Mr. Rudolph Ruzicka, one of the most skillful wood engravers now living, pointed out on seeing the object for the first time, the lines have been produced by a *pushed* stroke, rather than a *pulled* one which lacks control. They are clear-cut and not jagged; the intersections are sharp, and the stroke stays solidly on the line rather than swerving off. In other words, this is the work of a highly experienced artisan who had developed complete control of his technique and the medium in which he was working. He was an exceedingly skillful engraver, and not a beginner in any sense of the word. For this reason, it does not seem likely that the "sketch-book" hypothesis (see discussion on p. 24) legitimately can be evoked

16

to explain the drawings on the present object.

Both surfaces exhibit a maze of lines, predominately of U-shaped section and of inextricable appearance. In the entanglement, the following outlines have been deciphered:

Obverse Surface *(plate 2, no. 1 and fig. 1, no. 1)*:
(a) An extremely naturalistic male horse with characteristic roached mane and ladder pattern extending down the back (fig. 1, no. 2). This animal is remarkably expressive, and the facial details are clearly indicated. The forehead is slightly bulging, the mandible strong — almost square — and the lower line of the chest is slightly convex. The significance of the transverse line across the muzzle and the ladder pattern along the back is unknown. The neck is thick, all four legs are shown, and the sex is apparent. The club-like appearance of the hoofs is reminiscent of certain of the horses on the walls of the Cave of Lascaux (compare Windels, 1950, p. 61). Unfortunately the rump and tail have been broken off. In general appearance this horse suggests an animal similar to the living Norwegian Dun.

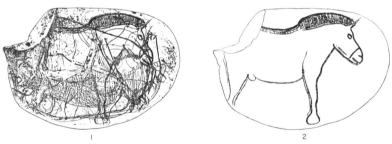

Figure 1

(b) Turning the pebble 180° one can easily discern the very finely drawn outline of a male reindeer (fig. 2, no. 1) with antlers shed and shaded underbelly. The animal's head is lowered to fit the curvature of the pebble in such a way that much of its mandible overlaps the muzzle of the horse. The nose, mouth, eye and ears are clearly shown, as well as the long hair along the lower side of the neck. The withers are raised in characteristic fashion, but the tail is not shown. All four legs are depicted, but the hind feet have been broken off and the front feet are lost in the superimposed horse's mane. The fact that this animal is shown hornless suggests that the drawing was executed during the winter months of the year.

(c) An ibex (fig. 2, no. 2) faces in the same direction as the reindeer just described. All but one of the animal's feet, which is partially complete, are overlain by the mane and back of the horse, while the forequarters are in turn surcharged by the head and neck of the reindeer. Again all four legs are shown, and the details of the head — mouth, nose, eyes, horns and ears — are clearly depicted. In this very realistic drawing the characteristic chunky, rectangular body and short tail of the ibex are faithfully expressed.

(d) An unfinished carnivore — possibly a bear (fig. 3, no. 1) — may be seen just to the rear of the ibex's head in the area of the reindeer's neck. The body of this animal is incomplete, with the exception of the neck, single foreleg and partially finished back, indicated by a double line. The line delimiting the animal's muzzle and ear is exceptionally heavy.

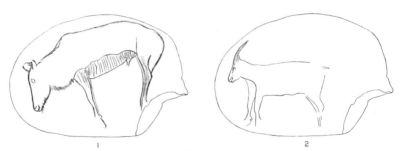

Figure 2

(e) Turning the pebble so that the horse is upright two animal outlines may be seen (fig. 3, no. 2). The forequarters and heads of both these beasts have been broken off. However, when separated out, their silhouettes suggest a cervid-like crea-

18

ture of some sort (fig. 3, no. 3) and a headless bison (fig. 3, no. 4). By combining certain lines shown in the area on the left-hand side of fig. 3, no. 2, with the outline of the latter quadruped, the Abbé Breuil has tentatively reconstructed a woolly rhinoceros, an interpretation with which the present writer does not agree. In any case, the subsidiary lines shown on the bodies of these two ruminants apparently indicate hair, and in the inextricable maze in the area to the left — just to the rear of the horse's hind leg — there is another ladder pattern similar to the one extending the length of the animal's back. Although other lines are discernible on this surface of the pebble, we do not feel competent to suggest their possible significance.

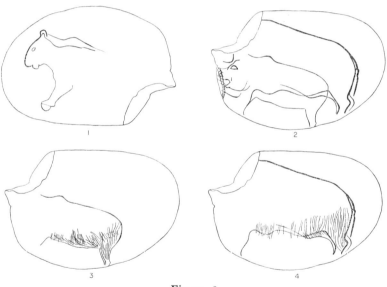

Figure 3

Reverse Surface *(plate 2, no. 2 and fig. 4, no. 1)*:
(a) The most outstanding single drawing on the reverse surface of the pebble found at La Colombière in 1948 depicts a woolly rhinoceros with lowered head, as if the animal were in

19

the act of grazing (fig. 4, no. 2). This figure is complete with the exception of the rear legs, which unfortunately have been broken off. Both front feet are shown, and the short hair or wool on the beast's underbelly is clearly indicated. The long, curved main horn and comparatively short rear horn are characteristic, and the eye is correctly placed in relation to the latter, judging by living rhinoceroses. Both the nostril and small mouth are easily discernible. This is the engraving of a singularly majestic beast, and it should be noted that the lines representing the hair or fleece on the neck, forelegs and massive shoulders have been cleverly arranged so as to suggest shading. As in the case of a finely sculptured figure, this is a thought expressed with greater vigor than is normally found in the case of Upper Palaeolithic engravings and paintings.

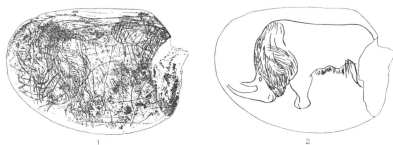

Figure 4

(b) In addition there are two incomplete drawings of woolly rhinoceroses facing in the same direction as the animal described above (fig. 5, nos. 1 and 2). Part of the back, shoulders, head, two horns, muzzle, nose and eye may be seen in the case of the former, the anterior horn and muzzle being indicated by an especially wide, deep line. The Abbé Breuil feels that the outline shown in fig. 5, no. 2, represents the back, head, eye and trunk of a mammoth, but this interpretation fails to explain the definitely associated horn, which is clearly the main horn of a rhinoceros and not the tusk of a mammoth. Therefore, we are inclined to consider both of the

20

drawings reproduced in fig. 5 as unfinished sketches of rhinoceroses — possibly attempts that were abandoned before the outstandingly fine engravings previously described were achieved.

(c) A partially complete second horse has been surcharged by the drawings of the rhinoceroses (fig. 6, no. 1). The rear quarters of this animal have been broken off, and neither the legs nor the line of the belly are shown. A series of short strokes indicates the line of the neck. The facial details are clearly indicated, the mandible is strong, and the height of the mane, which is suggested by a series of short forward sloping strokes arranged in a broad arc, is not limited. One has the impression that this is a different type of horse from the one shown on the obverse surface (fig. 1, no. 2). However, in com-

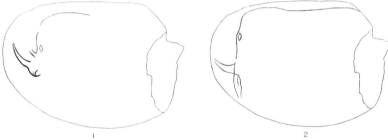

Figure 5

mon with the latter, a serpentine-like ladder pattern, which Breuil calls a "magical serpent," extends along the neck and part way down the back of the animal.

(d) Partially obscured by the complex of rhinoceroses is a second drawing, this one of a reindeer in absolute profile (fig. 6, no. 2). The antlers, if present, cannot be deciphered; a portion of the line showing the back of the neck and the withers is likewise missing, together with the feet and tail. Only three legs — two rear and one in front — are represented. The eye, indicated by a deep line, is disproportionately large, while the opposite is true of the mouth and nostril. As in the case of the reindeer on the obverse surface (fig. 2, no. 1), this animal's head is lowered as if it were in the act of grazing, and the long hairs on the undersurface of the neck and upper chest region are clearly shown. It is possible that the roughly parallel lines depicted on the lower jaw, throat and upper portion of the neck do not belong to this animal.

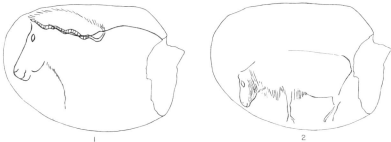

Figure 6

(e) In the vicinity of the group of the horse described above there is an area of diagonal shading (fig. 7, no. 1), the significance of which is by no means apparent. As shown in our drawing, there seem to be, in fact, two independent sets of these lines, one of which — the uppermost one in fig. 7, no. 1 — is similar to a series of diagonal lines enclosed by an oval line on the reverse surface of one of the engraved pebbles found at this site by Mayet and Pissot (1915, pl. XX, fig. 2) at this site in 1912. Breuil has suggested the possibility that this complex belongs to a human figure (fig. 7, no. 2), but he agrees that such an interpretation is exceedingly unlikely.

(f) Turning the pebble 180° one can discern a partially complete head of a carnivore of some sort (a felid?) in the upper central portion of the area (fig. 7, no. 3). Since we are uncertain with regard to the correct interpretation of this drawing, two possible versions of it are shown. In neither case are the lines strong and sure, indicating either poor technique or the fact that the hunter-artist had never had an opportunity of closely observing his subject.

(g) Finally, what is apparently a partially complete horse,

obscured not only by the rhinoceros but also by the horse described above, is shown (fig. 7, no. 4). The same curious slightly concave muzzle may be noted also in the case of one of the ruminants (possibly a wild ox) figured on the obverse surface of one of the older finds from this locality (Mayet and

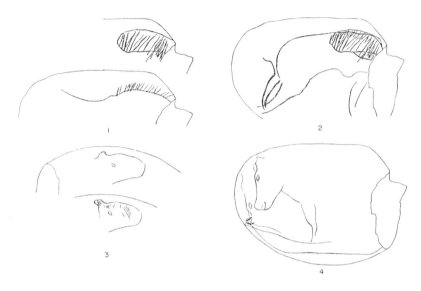

Figure 7

Pissot, 1915, fig. 43, p. 118). In addition, the back and head of a fourth horse may be seen by turning the object 180° (compare fig. 7, no. 4). This latter drawing, in which the animal's ears and right eye are indicated, is badly distorted by the curvature of the pebble. Apparently this engraving was never completed; it may have been abandoned since the artist attempted to execute it on an area where it must have been practically impossible to control the engraving tool.

Perhaps the most distinctive single attribute of the drawings on the pebble discovered at La Colombière in 1948 is the fact that their proportion is essentially correct. Furthermore, they are not stiff. Indeed they lack the clumsy awkwardness that characterizes the figures depicted on so many of the contemporary Upper Palaeolithic art objects. Finally, errors are singularly absent, with the exception of the two unfinished rhinoceroses on the lower surface. One may even note incipient attempts at perspective, and also the careful delineation of inner detail. It is at once apparent that the unknown person or persons who produced these drawings knew their models intimately at first hand — a fact which is reflected in the remarkably realistic portrayal of the forms represented. In particular the engravings of the horse, reindeer and ibex on the obverse, and the large woolly rhinoceros on the reverse are so remarkably alive and charged with energy that there is no mistaking the subjects. It may therefore be concluded that these pictures were drawn by a man, or men, who were not only exceedingly skilled engraver(s), but also knew the great animals well — knew the feel of their coats and the tremendous drive of their muscles, as well as the immense danger one faced while hunting them. Here, in short, is a product of advanced, highly developed creative thought. With a minimum number of lines a remarkably realistic series of animals seen in silhouette has been achieved. Not only is one dealing here with great technical skill, and keen power of observation, but also with the *desire* to reproduce, in a most difficult medium, the creatures upon whose existence Upper Palaeolithic man's economy depended.

The question naturally arises of the reason for the superimposition of so many animals on one object, such as the 1948 pebble. At first thought the idea of a "sketch book" seems obvious. But there are a number of objections to this, the most practical being that with a whole valley floor strewn with similar limestone pebbles, it would scarcely be rational for an artist to use just one to reproduce so many animals on the two surfaces of a small stone measuring 12 cm. x 8.2 cm. x 3.5 cm.

Another point is that were this a practice piece only, it would hardly seem possible that such near perfection could be attained for almost every drawing. There are practically no disoriented or inexplicable strokes. The artist or artists were obviously in perfect control of their media, and were far from needing practice in this case.

But with these rational, tangible explanations must go those which stem from the culture background against which we believe these prehistoric men lived. No known hunting peoples in the world today, or recorded in historic times, living under rigorous, exacting conditions, have ever practiced art for art's sake. And this was presumably just as true in the Old Stone Age. Such people do not draw, paint or carve merely for the sake of expressing themselves, or creating a beautiful picture, or even making records of the animals they hunted, although certain gifted members of the group may practice in order to develop their skills. In other words, art to them was basically a medium of expression for the purpose of propitiating in some manner the spirits of the animal kingdom. The form depicted was what had fundamental significance. If it was well drawn, that depended on the individual endowments and skill of the particular person who executed the engraving, painting, bas-relief or sculpture, as the case may be. For it is patently clear that if certain individuals who lived during Upper Palaeolithic times had not been endowed with a high degree of artistic ability, developed their technical skill to produce drawings, and possessed a true appreciation of aesthetic values, this ceremonial or magico-religious art could not have existed. The aesthetic urge plus the ability to draw had to be present in the case of the individual artist. However, it does not by any means follow that the forms which he created in giving expression to this urge were also regarded as works of art (*i.e.,* art as an end in itself) by the other members of his social unit — clan, extended family or tribe. Certainly to these people success in the hunt meant the difference between plenty and starvation, or near-starvation, just as in the case of modern hunting peoples living under comparable environmental conditions. On this basis, therefore, it seems difficult to avoid putting forward the suggestions that, in the eyes of the prehistoric inhabitants of La Colombière, this pebble was probably regarded as a hunting talisman rather than as an art object.

In view of these considerations, it seems probable that the use of a single pebble for the representation of so many animals was connected somehow with certain magico-religious rites pertaining to the chase. Thus we can imagine that the pebble was initially engraved and used in some sort of a hunting ceremony. Since that particular hunt was successful, the object was re-engraved and used on a subsequent occasion for the same purpose. It possessed magical qualities, or "mana." It is, therefore, tentatively concluded that the primary significance of this very fine object, from the point of view of the people who actually lived at La Colombière during the closing stages of the Ice Age, was not the beautiful engravings so carefully executed on its surfaces, but the fact that it was the medium by which it was possible to commune directly with the spirits of the animal world for the purpose of successfully replenishing the all-important food supply. And having served its purpose in connection with certain particular rites connected with the hunt, it was ceremonially "killed," as in the case of so many similar objects found in other sites of the same age in western Europe.

Since at La Colombière the drawings under discussion have been executed on an object small enough to be easily transported, they are certainly excellent expressions of *art mobilier*. But, together with such contemporary examples of a portable nature as the well-known series of artistically perfect statuettes and low reliefs from various European localities, they cannot be considered utilitarian in the strict sense of the term. In this respect, therefore, they should actually be compared with the wall or cave art group of Franco-Cantabria.

Now almost without exception this cave art is found in places that were perpetually dark, and there even seems to have been a preference on the part of the artists to choose the least accessible corners of the caves. For this reason, one is forced to conclude that the pictures were not primarily for decorative purposes. The fact that we are not dealing with art as an end in itself has been very clearly expressed by Breuil and Obermaier (1935, p. 13) with reference to the Cave of Altamira, near Santander, in northern Spain. These authorities state that this conclusion is even more evident "when we come to the fine engravings, which are hardly visible and generally can only be found with the greatest effort. These pictures, many of very indifferent exccution, but sometimes real artistic efforts, certainly owe their existence to the magico-religious idea, especially to the custom of hunting magic, as it is still practiced today among living primitive peoples. The fact that in more than one instance . . . . arrows or assegais were painted on the animals' bodies agrees with the magic theory, and is undoubtedly a sign of their being spellbound or of symbolic death. . . . Also it seems that certain places or corners in this cave and others must have been considered as especially sacred, and that the spells cast there were especially efficacious. Because of this, although in other parts of the cave there was plenty of available space, the artists repeatedly used the same places, piling their pictures one on the other, like palimpsests, not hesitating to destroy older ones, although they might be of great artistic value. One need not insist further that there may be an influx here of ideas of reproductive magic, or a cult of particular animals — totem animals. All this suggests that caves must then have existed dedicated regularly to a cult, since paintings are not to be found in every cave. . . . In each region, as far as one can see, there were few places of the same age that can be considered as real 'sanctuaries,' wherein no doubt Man celebrated ceremonies at which only certain (initiated) individuals might attend." Although we are dealing with a rock-shelter rather than a cave, and with engraved pebbles rather than with wall art, the question presents itself: Was La Colombière one of these sacred places in southeastern France during Upper Périgordian times? The answer is probably that it was not. In this case the engraved pebbles found at this site were more likely to have been a collection of possibly sacred objects belonging to the hunters who used the shelter during their seasonal visits. According to the geological evidence, the Ain River from time to time flooded its banks, and it is a valid conjecture that the collection was perhaps lost in some kind of flash flood which drove out the men in the shelter with time only to save their lives and not their possessions. Furthermore, judging by the paleontological data, the types of animals represented by the artists do not necessarily bear a direct relationship to the frequency of occurrence of the same species in the actual occupation layer. One therefore has the impression that the engravings were not necessarily actually executed at the temporary hunters' camp at the river's edge.

No discussion of the significance of Upper Palaeolithic art can be considered complete without some reference to the great classic painted caves of western Europe, such as Lascaux in the Dordogne region of southwestern France, and Altamira in northern Spain. It would clearly be idle to suppose that a rigid scheme of classification of the thousands of paintings and engravings found in these and other sites could supply us with a key to the riddle of Stone Age art. The compilation of a complete inventory and an exhaustive study of the details of each group of figures might provide some clue to their meaning, but this would be so vast a labor that it could only be accomplished in several lifetimes and by several highly competent and dedicated scholars.

The view that Lascaux—or Altamira—as a whole constitutes a single artistic unity, like a great cathedral, and that each craftsman who contributed his part placed his figures in relation to those already existing is inconsistent with the belief in an evolution of the artistic techniques employed. Various compositions and associations may be established, but the meaning of such combinations is still questionable. The dates when certain of the great painted caves were occupied by Upper Palaeolithic man have been established by Carbon 14 and other methods, but what is much more difficult to determine is the reason for their existence, the use to which primitive man put them, and what the groups of magnificently depicted animals meant.

In this connection, however, I think it is fair to say that ever since the beginning of Upper Palaeolithic times groups of food-gathering hunting peoples have practiced ceremonial magic to ensure either abundance of game or success in the hunt. Even today the Australian aborigines paint figures of animals and other signs on cave walls which have significance in connection with hunting ceremonies. And it is very probable that rites similar to theirs were performed in the depths of certain caves in western Europe, such as Lascaux and Altamira during Old Stone Age times. Thus one can imagine that the remote galleries of these dark underground labyrinths once witnessed witchcraft and ritual dances accompanied by the songs and cries of men in a state of trance. Such a hypothesis of spiritualistic or super-natural (magico-religious) significance of Upper Palaeolithic art explains a whole series of facts the meaning of which would otherwise be obscure. On this basis the stencilled or negative hands on certain cave walls may represent possession or power; the darts or javelins shown piercing certain animals would signify the desire to cast a spell on the game or symbolic death; masked human figures very probably were sorcerers or medicine men. However, with reference to this aspect of a stage in man's prehistoric cultural development, *which has forever vanished,* we can do no more than put forward hypotheses. In the final analysis, the only aspect of this problem which has reality is that our feeble attempts at interpretation and reconstruction are far behind the living reality as it was felt, thought and experienced by our very distant forefathers, with all that this implied in beliefs, faith and creative force. It is difficult enough for us to understand the mental outlook of a few historic generations ago: it is virtually impossible for us to turn our minds back into the limits of the intellectual experience and impulses of Périgordian and Aurignacian man.

Finally, it is as well to bear in mind that all systematics which may purport to explain a given sequence or development of Upper Palaeolithic art as a whole are simply working hypotheses —they are the formulations of the investigators, and *not* of the men who actually produced the paintings, engravings and sculptures under consideration.

The Abri Pataud Venus.

The Abri Pataud, in the medieval village of Les Eyzies, in the Dordogne region of southwestern France, is situated between the famous Crô-Magnon locality and the reconstructed Château des Eyzies which now serves as an archaeological museum. The site lies beside the main Périgueux-Sarlat road, and at the foot of the limestone cliffs facing west-south-west, that flank the Vézère River at this point. Actually the site proper is only one of a series of collapsed caves and rock-shelters, the ensemble of which constitutes one enormous series of occupations extending under the buildings of the present town. Its existence has been recognized for over sixty years, but due to the fact that the Pataud farm was located in the very center of the area, no really large-scale excavations were ever undertaken in the vast rock-shelter, although Emile Rivière did a small dig there at the end of the last century. In 1953 a test trench was sunk in the talus slope in front of the cliff, by the Peabody Museum of Harvard University. The results were sufficiently impressive to justify the purchase of the property, and the negotiations were finally completed by 1958 when excavations on a large scale were undertaken. The research is a joint Franco-American project under the auspices of the Musée de l'Homme in Paris and the Peabody Museum of Harvard University.

The first extensive occupation layer was unearthed during the removal of the *éboulis* and large limestone blocks which had collapsed from the overhang of the shelter during the last Glacial Stage. This layer, clearly referable to the Proto-Magdalenian, has been dated by the radiocarbon method at approximately 18,250 BC. It is extremely important in that it represents the only instance in western Europe, other than Peyrony's famous *Couche* F at Laugerie-Haute: Est, in which the Proto-Magdalenian has ever been recorded. From this level several human bones were recovered, the most significant being the skull and lower jaw of a young female, in an almost perfect state of preservation. It was found under a large fallen limestone block, protected by smaller stones around it.

Beneath the Proto-Magdalenian horizon a second level was discovered: that of the Final Périgordian. It contained a series of hearths, and water-worn pebbles, many of which had been cracked by heat. Obviously the latter had been carried up to the shelter by the prehistoric inhabitants, and may have had to do with cooking. There was also a rich fauna associated with this horizon, which consisted mostly of reindeer (90%; both *Rangifer arcticus* and *R. caribou sylvestris* occur), bovids, and horse (7-8%; more abundant than in the Proto-Magdalenian), cervids, chamois and ibex (very rare), fragmentary evidence of wild boar and fox, some rodents, birds (vulture and raven) and fish (salmon). Dr. Jean Bouchud, who has made an extensive study of the bones, states that the reindeer were killed throughout the entire year, proving that the site was occupied continuously, not seasonally. This is further borne out by the fact that there are no sterile layers in the hearths, and that almost all the Final Périgordian artifacts are made of local flint.

31

Besides the quantities of flint tools, worked bone and ornaments made of teeth and shells, several art objects came to light. The latter include the following:

(1) Fragments of bone exhibiting excised lines of vague geometric patterns, together with geometric engravings.

(2) A very curious example of an enigmatic "serpentine" pattern engraved on the inner (eastern) surface of a large block fallen from the shelter roof (plate 3). Most of the block was buried by the occupational débris of the layer.

(3) The most significant find from this horizon is a small bas-relief carving of a female figure (plate 4) which is described below.

Carved on an unprepared, roughly tabular limestone block 19 cm. long, 14 cm. wide and 5 cm. thick, the figure shown in low relief is almost exactly 6 cm. long and 1.1 cm. wide at the point of greatest width, namely at the hips. In comparison with other female statuettes and bas-reliefs from Aurignacian and Upper Périgordian sites in western Europe this carving apparently represents a comparatively young woman. Indeed the form is more slender and gracile than is usually the case. The lateral borders depicting the outline of the carving have been incised with great skill, although the cut surface scarcely extends over 10 mm. away from the left side of the figure; on the right side, however, it is not over 5 mm. wide. Apparently this variability results in part from the rough and uneven natural surface of the stone selected by the artist in the first instance. While somewhat more carefully finished and smooth, the actual surface of the carving itself is nonetheless rather rough, due in large measure to irregularities in the limestone.

The head, shown in profile turned at an angle of 90° over the right shoulder, is approximately 8 mm. in diameter. The highest point is near the bregma and from there the outline slopes off toward the occipital region. No trace of any of the facial features can be discerned. A raised area over the forehead and down over the ears apparently represents hair, but the hair itself is not indicated in detail. In the occipital region the neck is only vaguely detectable as a slight constriction between the base of the head and the very feebly-indicated left shoulder, but on the opposite side the throat is clearly and precisely defined. The shoulders, which are not pronounced, are falling and almost completely obscured by the breasts. No suggestion whatsoever of the left arm can be detected, but the outline of what appears to be a very vaguely indicated right arm may be noted in the groove that defines the individual's right side. It may well be, however, that this is simply the result of the fact that the grooved portion of the stone in this area has been incompletely finished, since a comparable situation exists in the region of the left hip that is definitely due to this cause.

The entire area of the thorax, which is some 11 mm. long and 10 mm. wide, is covered by the large pendulant breasts which extend down to the abdomen. One can clearly discern the separation of these very prominent features; it is in the form of an elongated V-shaped groove, the apex of which is immediately below the region of the ear. The breasts are asymmetrical: the left one begins higher up on the body than the right, so as not to obscure the throat area. Indeed, in a sense the former seems to be a continuation of the neck from just below the occipital region of the head. The medial border closely follows the line of the sternum, swinging off to the side along the line of the lower border of the rib case. In contrast with the right breast, it is fairly well filled, and in a downward direction it progressively augments in volume jutting out well beyond the individual's waist and completely masking the line of the side of the body. On the other hand, the right breast has its inception near the region of the clavicle—somewhat high but nonetheless approaching a more normal position — and it extends very slightly lower on the body than in the case of the left one. It is clearly outlined, but at the same time it is so pronouncedly flatter than the left one that, taken by itself, it could conceivably be interpreted as some sort of a short cut-away garment rather than as an anatomical feature.

The waist is slender, well-proportioned and delicate. It is 6.5 mm. in breadth and is the only portion of the figure that is really symmetrical. In comparison with the pronounced development of the breasts, which encroach on it from above, and the shield-shaped, rather distended abdomen which continues the outline of the lower portion of the body, the waist is of exceedingly reduced proportions. In profile it appears as a raised cylindrical-shaped feature between the breasts and the abdominal region, and it is at once apparent that in this area the concave lateral borders of the figure have been carved with considerable skill.

The upper (ventral) surface of the abdomen is slightly convex. The maximum breadth of this region, 10 mm., is almost exactly the same as that of the upper body, while the maximum length from the constricted region of the waist to the approximate lower border of the abdomen is approximately 11 mm. A possible indication of the navel can be detected. The abdomen is manifestly the most prominent sector of the individual's anatomy; indeed the degree of emphasis which the prehistoric sculptor has placed on this area makes it seem very probable that it was his specific intention to indicate pregnancy. Certainly the very narrow lines of the waist, the reasonable proportions of the hips, and the general slenderness of the lower limbs do not support the view that the prominence of the abdominal region is in fact the result of excess fat, as is manifestly true in the case of other female figures represented in Upper Palaeolithic art.

The groins are depicted by two fairly deeply incised, slightly curved lines, that are directed downward from near the region of the hips on either side of the body and intersecting at the line of the vertical axis of the figure. These lines form a broad V, and one can clearly observe a small horizontal line, some 4 mm. above the point of intersection, which delimits the upper border of the pubic triangle. Indeed the genital organs constitute a rather prominent feature. In a sense they are shown as a downward projection of the central portion of the abdomen from which they are delimited only by the light horizontal line mentioned above.

The lower limbs are shown in interesting fashion. From the region of the hips the cut away area that surrounds the entire figure extends downward, away from the head, in two long convergent furrows indicating the outline of the legs. This furrow is 30 mm. long on the right side from its junction with the line of the groin, while on the left it is very slightly shorter—28 mm. There is no indication whatsoever of either the knees or the feet. The division between the legs is shown in part by a very rough and ill-defined incised line that begins at the lower apex of the pubic triangle. This medial line ends just below the region where one supposes the knees of the model may have been located, and it has been made all the more irregular due to the presence of a very small dissolution cavity in the limestone in the region of the upper thigh. Several other small cavities of the same type are present on this surface of the stone, and all of them are quite free of any secondary crystalline formations.

Summary and Conclusions: This female figure, which has been carved on a completely unprepared limestone block, apparently represents a relatively young individual with a slender and graceful body. The dimensions are small: 6 cm. long by 1.1 cm. maximum width. The head is turned at an angle of 90° over the right shoulder, and whereas the features of the face are not indicated, the line of the hair is clearly shown. Although in the occipital region the back of the neck is only vaguely suggested, the chin and throat area in the front are very precisely defined. The shoulders are falling and almost completely obscured by the well-developed, pendulous breasts, which in large measure obscure the entire area of the thorax. Representation of the arms is considered doubtful. The slender and well-proportioned waist is clearly delimited between the pronounced outline of the breasts above and the markedly pear-shaped and rather conspicuous abdomen below, which continues the outline of the lower portion of the body. The abdomen is admittedly the most prominent feature of the body, and very probably it has been so rendered in order to indicate pregnancy. The pubic triangle is clearly depicted; approximately 4 mm. above the point of intersection of the two deeply incised lines that define the groins there is a small horizontal line which delimits the region of the genital organs from the main area of the abdomen. Two long convergent furrows indicate the outline of the legs, but neither the knees nor the feet are shown. Just below the region of the knees the roughly incised median line, which divides the legs, comes to an end. The left leg is very slightly shorter than the right, and a certain asymmetry can also be noted in the case of the breasts. Notwithstanding these slightly disharmonic features, however, the over-all proportions of the figure are both pleasing and at first glance symmetrical. Indeed, from a purely stylistic point of view, this figure has been rendered in the finest tradition of Upper Palaeolithic art as represented by the well-known series of carvings and statuettes, collectively known as Venuses, from various Aurignacian and Upper Périgordian sites in western Europe.

With this statuette and the several others from sites in western and central Europe and the U.S.S.R., the question naturally raises itself: what was the reason for their existence, for what purpose were they created? And this leads directly to a point of considerable significance in Palaeolithic art. Magnificent though the representations of animals are throughout the entire tradition of Old Stone Age paintings and engravings, there are almost none of the human form. And of these few, not one is executed with the apparent ease and simplicity which distinguishes the portraits of the beasts. Almost all are either masked as in the

36

case of the famous "Sorcerer" in the Cave of Trois Frères in southern France, or ineptly stylized as though drawn by a child, as in the group in the *puit* at Lascaux, or simply parts of the body, especially hands as in the previously mentioned cases. It would almost seem that there was a "tabu" against the reproduction by drawing or painting of the human figure. There was no such restriction, however, applied to carving in the round or in bas-relief of the nude human female figure. The majority of the small statuettes and engravings dating from Aurignacian and Upper Périgordian times are of recognizably female form, all are studied and many of them are obviously pregnant.

The purpose for which they were created can, of course, only be surmised. It is generally supposed that they had a magical intention and were part of some sort of human fecundity or fertility rite, as suggested by the excessive development of breasts, abdomen and buttocks in most of them. This hypothesis, however, is somewhat difficult to justify in view of the conditions of life of these prehistoric hunters. Economically speaking, the multiplication of a tribe would inevitably cause an increase in the competition for food, and this in turn would outweigh the advantage of greater numbers participating in the hunt. Furthermore, although the children could at distant maturity become of service to the hunters, they would meanwhile represent just so many more mouths to feed. This view is based on the attitude found among contemporary hunting peoples of Africa, Australia, Northern Eurasia and North America. While one can freely admit that these prehistoric men believed in sympathetic magic, to which they had recourse with regard to the reproduction of animals, the vital question remains: Did they attribute the same importance to the reproduction of their own kind? Personally, I feel that consideration of human fertility as an advantage to be sought and eventually provoked by the magical practices of the Aurignacian and Upper Périgordian hunters remains very problematical and unlikely.

In this connection, one should note that, in addition to these statuettes, over a dozen sites, especially in the Dordogne, have yielded a substantial number of engravings representing the female genital organs in a more or less schematic manner. Presumably these had just the same significance as the female statuettes, that is, symbolic of the reproduction of life, though not necessarily of any particular species. For this reason, one is inclined to see here the beginnings of the "Mother Nature" concept, which persists throughout the history of most primitive peoples. The symbol is female because of the regenerative factor, and is related to the eventual prosperity and over-all well-being of the group as a whole, rather than with the specific increase in the size of a given family within the social unit in question.

An erotic purpose has also been imputed to these engravings and statuettes, but there is no convincing argument either for or against this concept. In this connection Professor E. O. James (1957, pp. 146-147) has stated "these sculptured Venuses cannot be dismissed as 'the characteristic products of unregenerated male imagination' in view of their long history as an integral part of the cult of the Mother-Goddess in more advanced stages of civilization. An erotic element may have been inherent in the tradition, but the main purpose has been that of the promotion and conservation of life in ever-increasing abundance mediated in and through the outward signs of maternal fecundity long before the urge of life was personified in the Earth-Mother and her many and various counterparts in the composite figure of the Magna Mater of the Near and Middle East and in the Graeco-Roman world."

One may even suggest that these early hunters recognized life as a mystery, and to them the symbols of the human female reproductive organs were sacred because inherent in them apparently lay the supernatural power of generation. As Professor James says, "The woman being the mother of the race, she is essentially the life-producer, as her male partner is the begetter.

38

... But however essential in physiological reality the two partners may be in order to achieve procreation, the agent about whose maternal functions there can be no possibility of doubt is and always has been the woman. She is not only the symbol of generation but the actual producer of life. ... While in primitive society there has been some uncertainty about paternity, this element of doubt cannot obtain in the case of the mother. Therefore she and her organs and attributes have been the life-giving symbols *par excellence* ever since their first appearance in the Middle East and in Europe at the beginning of the Upper Palaeolithic. Her male partner was in all probability at first supplementary because his precise function in relation to conception and birth was less obvious and less clearly understood." (*loc. cit.,* pp. 152-153.)

In the final analysis, therefore, it seems to me that the source of this naturalistic art is threefold: *spiritualistic* in its foundation, *symbolic* in its application, and — one supposes — *magical* in the ceremonial of its ritual and incantations.

To sum up the content of this paper on the art of Upper Palaeolithic man in its many manifestations, it would seem that the most vital reason for its existence is that of Function. We have seen how primitive man in the modern world, living in underdeveloped and challenging conditions, does not employ art for its own sake. Rather, he makes it serve a purpose of his own in the propitiation of the gods of nature and of the chase. The expert in the group who produces the artistic expression for the group's needs may or may not be an outstanding creative craftsman. The result will be the same in the minds of the men who are dependent upon its use. An analogy may reasonably be drawn with the modern primitive and Stone Age man. The magnificent paintings, the fine engravings on bone and stone and the small female figurines all played a functional role. It is only by such an explanation that the over-all continuous picture becomes clear in any respect. The long tradition of artists all following one another, generation after generation, making their paintings and engravings often over those of the preceding era, however beautiful they may have been, served the same purpose: the assurance of the continuity of life by natural increase and by fortune in the chase. With our present knowledge this very general and very obvious line of speculation is the best explanation we can achieve of the dynamics which compelled our remote ancestors to create the indestructible and astounding forms of art which they have left for us to discover, examine and ponder over.

REFERENCES

Breuil, Henri *and* Hugo Obermaier. The cave of Altamira at Santillana del Mar, Spain; English text by M. E. Boyle. Madrid, Tipografía de Archivos, 1935.

James, E. O. Prehistoric religion, a study in prehistoric archaeology. New York, Praeger, 1957.

Mayet, Lucien *and* Jean Pissot. Abri-sous-Roche préhistorique de La Colombière, près Poncin (Ain). Annales de l'Université de Lyon, sér. 1, 39, 1915.

Windels, Fernand. The Lascaux Cave paintings. New York, Viking Press, 1950.

S. Kooijman
THE ART AREAS OF WESTERN NEW GUINEA

New Guinea is one of the largest islands in the world, rather a dwarf continent than an island. About half of it — the part west of the 141st meridian and the Fly River — is under the sovereignty of the Netherlands. It is the art of this area which forms the subject of this paper.

Art is man-made, and human society is greatly influenced by its natural surroundings, the land and its resources and the climate. A sketch of this inhospitable country is therefore necessary to provide a background.

Any relief map of Western New Guinea shows that a mountain range of alpine type crosses the middle of the island. From west to east the whole area north of the Central Mountains is hilly or mountainous and in many places rises steeply from the sea. The part of the island south of the mountains is lowland country, full of marshes, mosquitoes, and malaria, and crossed by numerous wide, sluggish, muddy rivers. In the wet season of southern New Guinea the whole of the low country is flooded, the villages being conveniently situated on hills. When I worked among the Marind-anim, I saw the dug-out canoes of the people lying at the foot of the hills in the dry season, seemingly useless but actually awaiting the flood like Noah's ark.

Snow-capped mountains are found in the Central Highlands — even rugged glacier-covered country in the Mount Carstensz complex, which is named after the Dutch sea captain Carstensz who saw its snowy peaks glistening in the sun during his exploration of New Guinea's southwest coast in 1625.

The valleys of the Central Highlands are the most densely populated part of the island, even though from either a New York or a Dutch point of view this density is not very impressive. In the western part of the Highlands are the Wissel Lakes, recently discovered from the air by the Dutch Air Force officer Wissel. The mountain Papuans subsist on horticulture, building solid fences to keep the pigs out of their gardens, which are also provided with a rather elaborate drainage system of ditches.

42

Their diet consists mainly of tropical tubers. Man's energy here is largely focussed on the acquisition of wealth in the form of pigs and shell money: material culture is poor and art is almost completely absent.

Unlike the mountain people, the Papuans living along the coasts and in the wide southern plains mainly subsist on sago. Meat comes from the pig (wild or domesticated), the cassowary, and the kangaroo. Smaller animals are not despised either, for instance the larvae found in the rotting trunks of the sago palm. Fish is caught in the sea as well as in the rivers and the marshes.

Even today, contact between the white man and the Papuan is often very superficial. In many cases it is restricted to a kind of silent barter; the Papuan receiving tobacco, steel axes, and clothes, and the white man getting pigs for food and carved wooden figures, bowls and utensils — the fascinating products of this rough culture dominated by art.

One must not overlook the Papuans of the Highlands. They are the pygmoid people, the normal height of the man being more or less equal to the normal stature of a European woman. The most important and spectacular part of the men's dress are the long penis calabashes, which are specially grown for the purpose. The women wear aprons. Their large carrying bags are worn over the head and the back, and are also used as a kind of mantle or cape.

The specific style areas can be defined against the background of these general cultural and geographical divisions.

The Northwestern Littoral

The islands in Geelvink Bay and the coasts of this inland sea form the central part of this style-area. To the west the Radja Ampat Islands, situated off the northwest coast of New Guinea, also belong to it. This fact, perhaps strange at first sight, is to be explained by the settlement of emigrants from Biak in Geelvink Bay, who moved westward from their poor and inhospitable homeland.

Taking into account the geographical position of the area, and the relations which have long existed between this mobile population and several islands of eastern Indonesia, it is not surprising to find that here one of the main motifs of ornamental art originates from the west. This is the scroll, which is used for works in various media — bark-cloth, wood, bamboo. The bamboo *plate 5* containers for tobacco and lime (for betel chewing) often show this type of surface ornament; the designs stand in relief against a shallow, darkened background. In wood the motif frequently occurs on neck-rests and on the handles of spoons and lime-spatulae.

The scroll is also used, in open work, in the elaborate plank-*plate 6* like prows of the huge, outrigged seafaring canoes; an integral part of such objects also being the human head. The rigid recti-linear form of this is typical of representations of the human head and the human figure in this area.

The same characteristics are found in the korwar, the spec-*plates 7-9* tacular wooden statuettes. (These also very often include orna-mentation of a scroll-like character.) The art-style of this area is so well typified by these objects, in fact, that it is often named the korwar style.

Korwar were made after the deaths of people who had been of social importance, for instance a village chief or the captain *plate 7* of a boat crew. They were also made for the beloved dead chil-dren of socially important people. In some cases the skull of the *plate 8* deceased was placed in the hollowed-out wooden head, while in

44

others (instead of there being a carved head) the skull rested *plate 7*
directly on the wooden body. The making of a korwar was the
work of a specialist who, of course, had to be an expert wood-
carver; it may also have been necessary for him to be a priest.
We are told, by one of the missionary writers, that the carving
of a korwar was performed by the *mon,* the priest who had a
special and close relation with the spirits. The act of carving
itself was by no means purely profane: it was accompanied by
the singing of sacred chants lamenting the deceased man for
whose spirit the korwar was made. His spirit was believed to
enter the wooden figurine. The contact which people desired
with the spirit was brought about by means of its dwelling-place,
the korwar, in a religious performance which was the *mon's*
task. When the advice and help of a deceased leader were
needed — for instance, in cases of sickness, at the beginning of
dangerous voyages — the priest would take the korwar in his
hands, incessantly calling the dead man's name. After some time,
the priest's hands would start to tremble. This trembling motion
would develop into a convulsive quaking, until eventually the
spirit, in full possession of the priest's body, would speak through
his mouth. These seemingly meaningless sounds would be interpreted as significant messages from the spirit world.

As long as the spirit in the korwar proved to be helpful in
protecting the living it was held in great respect. The korwar *plate 8*
was ornamented with strips of colored cotton and offered food
and tobacco. When, however, the korwar spirit proved not to be
helpful any longer, when the sick man died and the boat crew
did not return from dangerous foreign coasts, it was evident
that the spirit had abandoned the statuette. It was then merely
a worthless piece of wood which was either contemptuously
thrown away or hacked to pieces in anger.

What we know about two particular korwar in the collection *plates 8, 9*
of the National Museum of Ethnology at Leiden, Holland, may
serve to illustrate these remarks. One is about six generations *plate 8*

old: it was made at the beginning of the 19th century. Though collected in one of the Radja Ampat Islands, it was made on the north coast somewhere between the Geelvink Bay and the Radja Ampat Islands. Here the leader of a seafaring expedition died: these men were on their way from the island of Biak in the Geelvink Bay to the west. They took the korwar and also the spirit of their dead headman with them to assure themselves of his leadership and protection. The figure's headcloth indicates the high social standing of the deceased chief, as the right to wear such cloths was given by the Sultan of Tidore, in eastern Indonesia, to the so-called *sengadji*. These men were Papuan chiefs acting as links between the Sultan who claimed sovereignty over the area and the native population. They were also held responsible for the paying of the tribute required by the Sultan.

The attitude of the arms and hands of the statuette represents the invocation of Manseren Nanggi, the Lord of Heaven. This ceremony was performed by the eldest men of the community. In a way similar to the coming of the korwar spirit into the body of the priest, Manseren Nanggi was believed to take possession of his worshippers.

The attitude of the arms and hands of a second korwar is also *plate 9* strongly suggestive of the same religious ceremony. This figure was actually carved in the Radja Ampat Islands, the extreme western part of the style-area in question. Not surprisingly, it betrays Indonesian influences. The headdress should be noticed: it is probably the counterpart of a Portuguese helmet. Helmets of this type were brought into the Moluccas of eastern Indonesia by the Portuguese rulers, and have ever since subsisted in the area as ceremonial headgear.

The Northeastern Littoral

This area includes the stretch of the north coast of Dutch New Guinea between the mouth of the Mamberamo River in the west, and the political border in the east. The Lake Sentani region, located only a few miles south and southwest of Humboldt Bay, is culturally related to the coast. Indeed, Lake Sentani art and the art-forms of the coast have a number of elements in common. The former, however, evidences a characteristic style which is probably due to local development in a more or less isolated area.[1] Little information is available on the social function of art in this area. It is possible, however, to mention a few relevant elements of the culture as a kind of background to its art-style.

The inhabitants of this part of New Guinea's littoral are seafaring people. Their canoes, of vital importance to them both for fishing and traveling, are long, narrow dug-outs with one outrigger and a small platform on the wooden bars connecting the boat-hull with the outrigger. The gunwales are heightened by means of planks. The prows are provided with carved projections which are made in three types. The first is an S form, the upper *plate 10* part of which is a rather intricate composition of animals and humans. Other prow ornaments are V-shaped, and fastened by *plate 11* ropes to the V-shaped conjunction of the two gunwale planks. These ornaments are often based on the human head, carved in the traditional style of this area. The third kind of prow orna- *plate 12* ment consists of a more or less conventionalized representation of a bird. Unfortunately we have no information about the meaning of these objects; judging from the impression they make, however, these pieces of art probably belong to the mythical and religious sphere of life. Being indispensable attributes of the seafaring vessels, their dominating presence on the boat prows may in one way or another be of vital significance to the speed of the boat and the safety and success of its crew.

As in most Papuan societies, the human figure frequently occurs as a motif of wood-carving, whether as an adjunct to ceremonial objects, weapons, and utensils, or as a free-standing image. These figures do not convey any great emotion; with the rounded-off shape of the head, the body, and the limbs, they make an impression of restfulness and repose. This is perhaps

47

to be explained by the character of the culture, as life in these parts of the island was considerably less hard and merciless than among many Papuan peoples of the South and the South-west, where headhunting and murder continually harassed the population.

plate 13 This area is famous for its style of surface decoration, particularly on the bamboo tobacco-containers and on the lime-gourds. The basic design consists of an interplay of curvilinear figures, carved or burned into the surface. These display exquisite craftsmanship and a perfect mastery of material.

plate 14 Finally, we should remark the pottery of the area. It was built up from lumps of clay, the technique of the wheel being unknown in New Guinea. The designs were painted on free-hand. The pots were used for serving sago during feasts in which various clans took part. The designs on the pots—stylized representations of animals, particularly fishes—are the emblems of these clans, so that as the food was brought in, the feasting crowd could see from which group it came.

The Mimika Area

The Mimika area is the extreme western part of the large plain which stretches to the south of the Central Mountains. This belt of marshy and wooded country is relatively narrow here: it was indeed off this coast that Carstensz sighted the range now called after him. The land is intersected by a great number of rivers flowing from north to south. The people live on sago and fish, the sago palms being grown upstream in the tropical jungle, while most of the fish are caught in the mouths of the rivers. Hence the mobility of the Mimika people, who continually move up and downstream in their dug-out canoes.

Spectacular ceremonies form an essential part of this culture, as is indeed true of many cultures of the great southern plain, which are characterized by elaborate dramatic performances of masked dancers. It holds good for the Asmat, for the Marind-

48

anim, as for the Elema and other peoples of the Gulf of Papua.

Generally speaking, Mimika art is closely connected with ceremonial life. The most spectacular ritual objects of art are the *mbitoro* or spirit-poles (*mbi*=spirit). These are carved out of a huge tree with a number of plank-like connections between the trunk and the roots, all of which are chopped off but one. This root is elaborately carved in open-work, so as to form a kind of wing-like extension at the top of the pole. The pole itself is hollowed out almost completely, into the form of one or more stylized human figures of which only the heads are fully represented, the body and limbs being merely indicated in the carved-out cylindrical wall. These objects have a rectilinear, irregular surface ornamentation which is typical of the area, and are completed by being painted in white, black, and red.

The significance of the *mbitoro* is revealed by both their name and their shape. The latter is closely connected with the Papuan conception of the soul. This is by no means a purely spiritual matter, for it is believed that at death the soul leaves its dwelling place together with the "inner body" with which it is identified. Only the *kao*, the lifeless cover, is left. To the Papuan these "hollow" human figures are therefore quite literal representations of deceased persons, and well-known persons at that, since every figure is given the name of the man it represents.

The *mbitoro* were made for the boys' initiations, the highlight of which consisted of the nose-piercing ceremony, the poles being planted in front of the special houses built for the purpose. Judging by their position on the festival grounds they were apparently intended to emphasize the sacred traditional character of the ritual, at the performance of which the whole community—both the living and the dead—should be present.

The human body carved in *mbitoro*-style may well be called the dominant motif in Mimika art. This may be illustrated by examples of other objects. A drum, a fine specimen of native *plate 15* craftsmanship, shows a handle which has been executed in this particular style. The style persists in modern crucifixes, now frequently encountered all over the area, since Christianity in its Roman Catholic form is today the official religion of the whole population. They are hardly crucifixes in the actual sense, but a hybrid form: the product of the process of blending of native religion with Christianity.

plates 16, 17 Two types of masks occur in the area, both consisting of a framework of rattan and a rope-plaited cover of the head and the shoulders. Large fringes of leaves hang from the rattan hoops to form a costume covering the lower part of the wearer's body. The men who wear the masks represent recently deceased individuals of some importance, for instance a war leader, a popular village chief, a clever hunter. The ritual in which the masks play a leading role is held in order to ensure that the spirits of the deceased in question will retire satisfied and content to their abode far away in the mountains.

This feast is called: *mbii kawané* (spirit platform). Real platforms are erected in the morning on the edge of the open ground facing the forest behind the village. Towards the end of the afternoon a growing tension makes itself felt among the assembled crowd. All at once masked performers emerge from the edge of the forest. These "spirits" wildly toss the fringes of their masks into the air, wave their arms and totter about like drunkards. (However, they are careful in crossing the slippery ground not to lose face by landing in the mud.) The village headman, dancing on the edge of the open space, advances a short distance to meet the spirits. The older men shout and caper about to make the coming of the spirits as terrifying as possible. After the spirits have climbed on the platform, a passionate weeping breaks out. The impersonators of the dead are then invested with the attributes symbolizing their particular skill and high social standing during their lifetime. A great hunter, for instance, will get a pig spear put into his hand. He will then brandish the weapon, challenging the living by saying: "Which

50

of you is as good at pig hunting as I used to be?" The challenge is taken up by the village headman who emphasizes the fact that the deceased has been a great hunter indeed, but that his place has been taken by others who are at least as good as he, and that there is plenty of food in the village. In other words: "You have been great, but we can manage without you. So, please do not stay with us." After some time, someone whispers to the spirits: *"Hari-ja"* ("It is enough"). The masked men then return to the forest, crossing the open space to the accompaniment of shouts, shrieks and loud wailing. After the ceremony is over people feel quiet and comfortable: "Now the dead are satisfied," one of the guests said, "now we can go everywhere, into the woods and up the river without fear of being made sick. We have honored the dead. We feel contented and cheerful. Now we can let the dead rest."

Colorfully painted bark-cloth skirts also belong to ceremonial life. They are worn by the women as festive dress when waiting for the boys, taken away from them for initiation, who are on the point of emerging from seclusion.

The *yamaté* objects are ceremonial as well. Shield-like in form, they have a carved surface ornamentation which is very complicated and, in most cases, asymmetrical. The *yamaté* are displayed at the Iamakané feast. They are either standing in a row in front of the house or hanging on its wall, at first completely hidden by a cover of mats. These are removed all at once in the course of the feast. The women whom the *yamaté* are meant to impress then duly give vent to their admiration.

Besides these ceremonial works of art, there exist traditionally ornamented objects for everyday use: paddles with carved blades, food bowls, and canoe prows. Two types of prows may be men- *plate 18* tioned; both are carved in open-work. The first has a fine minute though thoroughly irregular pattern. The second is also irregular, but is stronger and far less complicated. Such prows are not to be found in the area any longer. As with many of these wonderful pieces of Papuan craftsmanship, they are things of the past only to be seen in museums.

The Asmat Region

The Asmat live along the broad muddy rivers and in the marshy forests southeast of the Mimika, in one of the most isolated and inhospitable parts of New Guinea. They live mainly on sago and fish and their way of life is semi-nomadic. They group themselves, it is true, in villages of some size (five to fifteen hundred persons) but these communities have no permanent character. They move over considerable distances, and at irregular intervals, within a certain area.

The inhospitable character of this mud-covered, malaria-stricken tropical jungle was pretty well matched by the character of its inhabitants. Headhunting was a national sport, and still is except in the areas which are now under government control. Strangers are very much distrusted. When they are weaker, like the neighboring Mimika groups, headhunting raids and attacks are made upon them. Contact with stronger outsiders (such as Europeans) is avoided as much as possible.

This accounts for the fact that the Asmat, their culture, and their magnificent art were practically unknown until after World War II. Some ten years ago, however, the impact of Western civilization began to make itself felt. European government officials, missionaries, and traders were then confronted with an art-style which certainly equalled the already well-known styles of eastern New Guinea. From then on, specimens of Asmat art started to enter museums, arousing the admiration and interest of both art-lovers and ethnologists.

plate 19   The basic form of the tremendous number of anthropomorphic objects and ornaments in Asmat art is the wooden statuette representing a squatting man or woman with drawn up knees and bent arms and hands raised to the chin. The position of the limbs determines the characteristic shape of the figure, while

52

other stylistic traits are the longitudinal grooves on the outside of the arms and the legs which in several places are broken up by transverse or slanting "bridges." Besides these rather naturalistic squatting figures there also exist more or less strongly conventionalized sculptures.

Even certain utensils take human form, for instance the oblong *plate 20* wooden bowls for serving sago and that particular dainty, the sago larva. Here the boat-shaped dish is the hollowed out body. Here also full emphasis has been given to the limbs, which are represented in the same characteristic way as in the free standing figures.

The latter are rightly designated by the term "ancestor figures." The ancestors occupy a very important place in the people's thoughts, and in some way they are believed to be present in all sorts of objects of ritual and secular daily use. Most statuettes, shields, sago bowls and so on, are therefore given personal names.

This ancestral character is clear in the human figures forming part of the large ritual poles, the *bisj*. As with the *mbitoro* of the Mimika, the *bisj* consists of a tree trunk with an extending plank-root. After having been cut in the forest the tree is floated to the village between the long dug-out canoes. It is then brought to an annex of the men's ceremonial house where the actual carving is done by artists who are recompensed with food.

The most essential part of the *bisj* seems to be the boat-shaped shaft. Thus the human figures and the open worked plank-like extension should be interpreted as an elaboration of the prow ornament which has been developed at the cost of the boat proper. In all probability the *bisj* is essentially a soul-ship, the vessel in which the spirits of the deceased make their journey to the realm of the dead: which may also explain why some *bisj* have been found lying on the ground with paddles along their sides. One of the purposes of the ritual performed round the *bisj* is therefore the driving out of the dead. The dead, represented by the human figures of the *bisj*, are all of them important members of the village who fell in enemy raids. Another important aspect of the ritual is therefore the confrontation of the living with the images of the dead in order to arouse vengeful feelings. These feelings are immensely stirred by war-dances performed by the men and by sham attacks on the *bisj*.

More or less similar in function are the *uramun* which have, however, a far more clearly boat-like appearance than the *bisj*. The prow of the *uramun* resembles the prow of a real war canoe. The sitting figures represent bird-like beings *(ambirak)*; human beings are often found as well. The central figure is a tortoise. The *ambirak* and the human figures represent the spirits of men and women who have met a violent death. They are bidden farewell during the *emakatsjem* ritual which is centered on the *uramun*.

However, this ritual and the *uramun* have yet another quite different aspect: they are essential for the initiation of the young boys. The boys are secluded for about three months in a special building. Its gabled roof is provided with a heavy ridge-pole which protrudes from the front of the house. The end of the pole is carved with the head of an animal, probably a mythical monster. The building as a whole is indeed considered to be a monster: it will move sometimes (when the men make it shake on its poles), and it may even growl and roar. The boys, having been devoured by the monster, are given back at the actual initiation. One after another they emerge from the house, they come down the ladder, and are made to sit down on the central tortoise of the *uramun,* which has been placed in front of the house. There they are given the scarifications which mark them as adults. The significant role of the tortoise figure in this initiation ceremony is to be explained by the fact that the animal is a symbol of fertility on account of the many eggs it produces.

Two-dimensional art is largely dominated by more or less stylized representations of the human figure. This may be shown by the patterns carved on the bamboo headhunting horns. These are blown at the time when a victorious war-party is returning to the village. The number of horns blown on board the approaching canoes equals the number of heads taken by the men. Each horn having its own pitch, the women know before the actual arrival of the men how successful the raid has been.

The captured head is opened at one side by fracturing the temporal bone with a special kind of stone axe. This is done in order to facilitate the removal of the brains, which are eaten, as are other parts of the body. While the skull is still fresh it is given to an uninitiated boy who has to sit days at a stretch with the blood-covered skull between his legs, staring at it without moving or showing any sign of emotion. This will help to make him a fearless warrior and ruthless headhunter. The skull is afterwards ornamented.

The man represented by one particular mask was a renowned *plate 21* headhunter during his lifetime. This is shown by his ear ornaments: the wearing of cassowary feathers and coix seeds is the privilege of the successful warrior. The wooden nose-ornament imitates the bone the living men wear through the septum. Wooden frames are fastened to the eye-holes of the mask. These taper into a beak, probably a hornbill's, for according to myth this bird often flies to the "land beyond the water," the realm of the dead.

This man is Aipas, the village headman of Atat in the western Asmat area. He got exactly what he deserved, for he himself was killed and beheaded. This happened in 1948. A few years later the mask was made to be used during the *yipai* ritual. One of the purposes of the ceremony was to give a new father to the orphans of the man the mask represents. The new father wore the mask, thus indicating that he took the place of the dead. The children danced round the masked man, their new father. Afterwards the new relationship was publicly confirmed by the exchange of food, one party giving sago, the other fish.

To return to the subject of surface ornamentation, we may notice the stylized patterns on openwork spear-shafts. This pattern is rather intricate. It consists of a stylized representation of two squatting figures sharing a single head. This one is still more conventionalized, but its basic form is clearly visible, namely the human body with bent arms and drawn-up knees.

plates 22-24 The Asmat shields, which are about as high as a man, are usually cut from the plank-root of the same kind of tree from which the *bisj* are made. The front is covered with a carved pattern painted in red, white, and black. Here too the human figure is the principal motif, sometimes in the form of a number of disconnected arms and hands. It seems likely that these are intended to avert danger, for by raising their arms and stretching out their hands, the Asmat people try to protect themselves from strange and unknown dangers. White men entering the area have often been confronted with large groups of people using this kind of Papuan deterrent. The gesture was accompanied by cries of *"Papisj, papisj,"* which meant that *papisj* (a legalized and temporary exchange of women by the married men) should be practised in order to restore the cosmic equilibrium which had been disturbed by the coming of the strangers.

The patterns carved on the blades of the long paddles are very similar to the usual ornamentation of the western Asmat shields: long curves consisting of two ridges with a groove in the middle which is "bridged." These grooves and the "bridges" remind us of the decoration on the outer side of the arms and legs of the wooden statuettes. The human figure is therefore probably also the origin of this type of surface ornamentation.

plate 25 Shields from the region south and southwest of the Asmat area show a different style. Some from the Awju tribe and from the Muyu area can easily protect five or six men. They are used for attacking a house or a group of houses. A strut at the back holds the shield upright while the attackers throw their missiles from its shelter. At the right moment they move on behind the shield as Roman soldiers approached the walls of a besieged city under cover of the testudo.

The Marind-Anim

The Marind-anim live in southern New Guinea, on the sandy coast and along the rivers in the inland country; but the coastal area is the centre of Marind life. Most of the people live there, food—coconuts and sago—being plentiful.

The more or less permanent settlements of the coastal people are on the low ridge of dunes behind the beach. This is indeed the only place safe from water in the rainy season, which lasts from December to June; during these months the whole lowland area behind the coast is flooded. For that reason the Marind raise their garden-beds so in the wet season the latter seem to float on the water. They are consequently called *yavun*, boats. In the dry season people used to take to the dried-out plains behind the coast to live a semi-nomadic life of hunting and roving about for months.

The cultural pattern was dominated by two factors, the great tribal festivities and headhunting. While in a material sense Marind culture was poor (even axes, clubs, and arrows were traded from the neighboring tribes), ceremonial life was highly developed and abundantly rich.

As in most primitive societies, artists formed an integral part of the community. They did not care for decorating the simple weapons and utensils, but concentrated on adjuncts to the culture's real interests, namely the attributes of the headhunting party and the paraphernalia of the great ceremonies.

According to the Marind themselves, they went headhunting "because there were no names left in the village." Every Marind child was given several names, the most important being the so-called head-name, the name of a killed and beheaded enemy. So when people needed head-names the necessary preparations were made. A new men's house was built. The *kuiahat* (head-

57

fork), which played an important part in the headhunting complex, was placed in the middle of the house. The *ayassee,* the headhunting song, was sung as the men danced round the *kui ahat* for days. When they set out on the actual campaign the *kui ahat* was carried as a kind of standard. The target was always some village in the area of a neighboring inland tribe, the approach to the village taking place during the night. Shortly before daybreak, it was completely surrounded. All at once the houses were set on fire and the attackers started to shout. The villagers tried to escape into the woods, but most of them were captured. Children as a rule were not killed, but taken home and adopted as a welcome addition to the tribe's declining numbers. Men and women were taken alive. They were at first soothed so that they should tell their names (the sound or cry uttered by the bewildered victim was considered to be his name); these were afterwards given as "head-names." Then the actual killing and beheading took place: the flesh of the neck was cut through by means of a sharp bamboo knife. By twisting the head the spine was broken, and the head separated from the body. The heads were prepared later. The skin was carefully removed and dried on a fire and the skull cleaned of brains and flesh. Then the skull was padded with clay and the dried skin was pulled over it. Rope-like plaited hair ornaments *(mayub)* were attached. The wearing of *mayub* is the privilege of the adult men and women, and they vary in size according to the sex and the age-class of the wearer.

When the war-party returned, the heads were hung either on *plate 26* kui ahat or on the *ahat dema.* The latter also played an important *plate 27* part in headhunting. A *dema* is a mythical hero who lived "in the beginning" and whose feats are reproduced in dramatic ceremonies. The significance of hanging the captured heads on the upraised arms of this *dema* must have been clear to all, as the *dema* was the god of the netherworld.

The great tribal ceremonies mainly consisted of elaborate

dramatic scenes in which the *dema* made their appearance. The sacred events were reproduced on the fenced-in festive grounds: a matter of vital importance to the well-being, even the survival, of the community. These performances were by no means mere amusement: arousing feelings of reverence and awe, they made the people participate in the origin of human life and human institutions.

The actors in these performances were spectacularly adorned. Being meant only for a long distance effect, the objects with which they were bedecked are often poorly executed. They are made of very soft wood and often give the impression of being improvised.

A type of mask, made of sago leaf-sheath, represented a *heis,* the ghost of a dead man. Compared with the elaborate masks of the Mimika and Asmat Papuans it is particularly plain and simple. Horn-like extensions on the head are probably a stylization of the arms of the *ahat dema.*

Fine pieces of native craftsmanship were the bull-roarers used during sacred rituals. By swinging them around on a long rope a buzzing sound was produced. To the uninitiated—the women and the children—this was the voice of the spirit of the men's house.

The drums which played an important part in the feasts and *plate 28* ceremonies were most of them beautiful solid pieces which were sometimes longer than a man's height. They were made by the inland-Marind and acquired by the coastal people by barter: a typical example of good craftsmanship not being a part of Marind life in its essential aspects, the celebration of the sacred rituals and the dramatizing of the feats of the *dema.*

---

[1] S. Kooijman, The Art of Lake Sentani. New York, The Museum of Primitive Art. 1959.

59

George Kubler
RIVAL APPROACHES TO AMERICAN ANTIQUITY

Today two kinds of collectors compete for what is usually called primitive art; they are the social scientists, and the art collectors. The nature of these two groups, both acquiring works of art in the same classes, but for such different purposes, marks out the measure of the difference of approach.

I shall limit myself to American antiquity, when peoples of an astonishing diversity lived and flourished during about the same span of time as the peoples of the ancient Near East.

On one side are the anthropologists, who, as the leading students of American antiquity, have generated methods and principles quite different from those of the art museum curators and historians of art. Their interests as art people in these materials, though less systematic, is at least as old as the anthropologists', as we shall see. The rival approaches, then, are those of the natural history museum, where the anthropological study of American antiquity reigns supreme, and the art museum, where conceptions about *quality* govern the study of the same objects.

Only their works tell us about these ancient peoples. We deduce that some were simple villagers. Others were priestly rulers or professional warriors and their subjects. A few literary sources of preconquest date confirm these rarefied deductions. Occasionally a city like Chanchan speaks to us of complicated *plate 29* dynastic politics. Piedras Negras was surely a courtly center of exquisite refinement. But beyond these affirmations we cannot reconstruct any web of events without written records. Chanchan came into being without benefit of writing. More than half of the written signs of Maya civilization still are undeciphered. Occasionally the traces of an identifiable individual artist are legible in the sculptures of Palenque or in the pottery portraits of the north coast of Peru. Hence the artistic identities are remote and unclear: they emerge indistinctly from the works, but if it were not for these works, we could not apprehend personalities at all.

Our scope embraces only the principal urban civilizations of ancient America, from the Tropic of Cancer to the Tropic of

Capricorn, in a quadrant as wide as from Lisbon to Istanbul, and as high as from Cairo to Leningrad. It lies upon the latitudes of Central Africa, about equal in size to western Europe. As in western Europe, the coastlines define several seas, but the American land area is far smaller, and its river systems separate the regions more than they connect them. Much of the land surrounds a great Atlantic body of water, of which the western (Gulf of Mexico) and the eastern (Caribbean Ocean) parts are analogous to the eastern and western Mediterranean, with Yucatan like an Italian peninsula.

It is instructive to rank the main regions of American antiquity by the reliability and the exactness of our chronological knowledge. Maya studies lead the field, because of the incomparable epigraphic material carved upon buildings and relief sculpture. Many archaeological ties allow Mexican materials to be dated in relation to the Maya series, and there are reliable texts of preconquest origin which pin down the events of the last few precolumbian centuries. Lowest in the order of chronological fineness and credibility are the Andean sequences, where only gross relations are sure, but not the intermediate positions within a stylistic sequence. It is as if we knew only that Carolingian art preceded the Renaissance, but not how many centuries intervened, or whether the sequence was valid for Spain and England too.

Deductions of this sort nevertheless color our understanding of the American past very deeply with exaggerated hues and contrasts. For example, the prevailing division of antiquity by preclassic, classic, and post-classic eras corresponds in most investigators' minds to a sequence of stages in the economic and political organization of the American Indian peoples. Pre-classic time, prior to the Christian Era in our normal chronological thinking, was the age of early village societies; the classic era witnessed the rise and fall of theocratic states; and in the post-classic period, feudal aristocracies appeared, under dynastic rulers engaged in military expansion. The pattern is assumed to be the same wherever large urban populations thrived, with only minor variations of terminology, such as the term "florescent" which means the same thing in Andean studies as "classic" in Maya archaeology. The American evidence is sometimes instructive about stages on which Old World archaeology has little to say. An example is the architecture of the ritual concourse center, for which Maya and Mexican examples are abundant. Old World examples are few and incomplete, like Stonehenge or Avebury.

We have no alternative to offer for this grand neo-evolutionary scheme: probably the early American civilizations did not evolve very differently from those of the Old World. Our principal question should be aimed at the methods of arriving at this knowledge. It is a striking fact that the study of Old World antiquity was from its beginnings in the Italian Renaissance a branch of humanistic learning, while New World antiquity, which has been systematically studied only since about 1850, soon became a scientific pursuit, more closely related to anthropology than to humanistic studies.

Today an archaeological report on an American site is a "scientific" production of graphs, statistics and impersonal language purporting to reach proven and repeatable conclusions. Such a report has nothing to do with the interpretation of literary works. On the contrary, philology has almost been forgotten by archaeological science. Where the excavation finds are unblessed by writing, philology entirely disappears. Indeed, the "scientific" connections of archaeological work, whether in Europe or America, increase as the material culture under study approaches "primitive," i.e., non-literate art.

Hence archaeology in America joins with "ethnology" (the study of living peoples) and with linguistic science as a section of anthropology, dedicated to the study of "primitive" peoples. Archaeology is a scientific technique rather than a fully autonomous discipline. It is important whenever documents fail to yield direct evidence of the past, and in the hands of the anthropologists, it is applied to the recovery of information about social structure and economic life. In this context works of art are used as sources of information rather than as expressive realities.

What kind of information does the anthropologist want from archaeological objects? If I may presume to simplify his thoughts, his information conforms to twin guiding principles. In the first place, culture is real, and the objects connected with a culture possess a linkage given by its reality, by its *reification,* by its having been constituted through an act of the mind into a *thing* with the illusion of physical, measurable properties. In the second place, the anthropologist resists the idea of separate origins for the same item of behavior, and he prefers to regard any cultural product as the result of a process of diffusion.

In the attempt to study the whole configuration of culture, anthropological science has been concerned with aesthetic activity only as a component of culture. The question at once arises whether "culture" indeed "includes" aesthetic activity. The anthropologist usually assumes that every aesthetic choice made by the members of a culture must be determined by that culture itself. But when we apprehend any culture as a whole, its axioms or postulates resemble aesthetic preferences. Thus two peoples living under similar environmental conditions may exhibit contrasting attitudes in respect to the total ordering or integration of their lives. At every point in the long, unconscious adaptation to environment, people have the faculty of choice. They can reject some alternatives, and accept others, more often than not for reasons of pleasure and dislike rather than necessity. To be sure, many persons' choices are conventional, but we are here discussing the significant choices of the minority elite whose decisions become conventions. In all epochs, artists have been foremost in channeling the future along these fateful ways of pleasure and displeasure.

The history of art cannot entirely be included by anthropological science, despite the fact that the history of art treats only a fraction of the material culture which is a main object of anthropological research. Anthropological conclusions about a culture do not automatically account for the art of that culture. As Jakob Burckhardt long ago remarked, on the state as a work of art, the culture itself can be regarded as an aesthetic product, brought into being by the same non-rational choices that mark a work of art. On the other hand, the work of art is of course incapable of being made to explain all of the culture in which it was produced. No explanation of culture ever fully accounts for its works of art because aesthetic activity lies in part outside culture, and it is anterior to culture as a possible agent in the processes of change.

Another consequence of the reification of culture by anthropologists is the rigid evolutionary scheme of cultural development in fashion since about 1950. If culture is a real entity, then its existence in time must have had segments, separated by determinable historic dates.[1] This kind of thinking is familiar enough in historical studies, where numerous documents require a nuancing in the artificial device of historical periods. In archaeology, however, the temptation is always present, to adjust the durations to preconceived ideas of their content.[2] For example, the style of pottery painting found at Tiahuanaco in Bolivia reappears throughout the central Andes, seeming to displace earlier local manners. No texts explain these events, and archaeologists have felt free to suppose (a) that the Andean diffusion of the style corresponds to military conquest or religious conversion by *plate 30* a dynamic tribe residing at Tiahuanaco, and (b) that these events occupied a narrow span of time after 1000 AD in the post-classic era. Today, however, more and more lines of evidence converge to suggest that the center of diffusion was not at Tiahuanaco but in the Mantaro basin, and that the spread of the style lasted many centuries, antedating the putative "expansionist" period and beginning even in pre-classic time.

In short, ceramic frequencies give reliable information only about very coarse time relationships: about the history of the

66

craft itself; and perhaps about economic conditions if other evidence is available. But sherd frequencies are unsatisfactory evidence for political or sociological reconstructions. Pottery sequences reflect other orders of events only after delays and with much levelling of a more agitated reality. If we had to rely upon ceramic history alone for our knowledge of Hellenic events in the period 550-450 BC, the shift from black-figure to red-figure painting would probably be interpreted as a political or sociological event rather than as a craft transformation.

The other main theme in recent anthropological discussion concerns the diffusion of culture from the Old World to the New. Two schools of thought are present: the diffusionists, who exclude the possibility of independent invention; and the school of Americanists who defend the thesis of independent origins for New World civilizations. Diffusionism has had defenders since the sixteenth century, when the lost tribes of Israel were invoked to account for the racial origins of the American Indian peoples.[3]

The thesis of independent origins first was stated in the 1840's, by F. Kugler in Germany, and by J. L. Stephens in the United States.[4] Both men independently destroyed the arguments for Old World origins of American Indian art by demonstrating the autonomous and self-contained character of the principal artistic traditions, and by showing that resemblances to the arts of other regions of the world, such as India or Egypt, could be explained as convergences rather than as borrowings by Americans from Old World sources.

More recently, the topic was dormant for a generation, from about 1925 to 1950, when the thesis of the independent origins of the New World civilizations was the orthodox view among North American archaeologists, working mainly under the leadership of A. V. Kidder at Carnegie Institution of Washington. Their hypothesis was that America received its first settlers from northeast Asia near the close of the last ice age, and that migration was thereafter cut off by physiographic changes at Bering

Strait. All American Indian civilizations were believed to have developed independently upon this palaeolithic base without further influences from the Old World. The hope was to prove that the human species, if cut off in a favoring environment near the beginnings of history, would spontaneously develop cultures parallel to those of the other races of mankind, but owing nothing to them by way of historical influences beyond the original palaeolithic fund of knowledge.

The independent inventionists have never denied the occurrence of small-scale intermittent migrations from Asia or Europe, like those of Scandinavian sailors after 1000 AD to New England and the Great Lakes. But they have rightly regarded these episodes as insignificant in the large framework of indigenous development. More important is the absence of major Old World traits from the technological repertory of the New World peoples: traits such as horses and large wheeled vehicles. The diffusionists have not provided any explanations of these absences.[5]

This question of the origins of American Indian civilizations remains one of the great questions in world history. It is still an open question. The linked sequences of Old World history afford no opportunity to verify the thesis of distinct cultural traditions arising from independent origins. Only America provides the possibility of establishing a case for independent invention. We must therefore weigh with extreme care any assertion pretending to resolve the issue. We cannot here test the racial and agricultural evidence, but we should be prepared to question the visual comparisons upon which the new diffusionists have based certain recent arguments.[6]

For example, Ekholm has supposed that a center of Asiatic influences flourished after the eighth century AD on the western border of the Maya peoples, bringing into Mesoamerica traits imported from the art and architecture of southeast Asia. For nearly every one of these forms, however, still other Old World origins can be suggested. The trefoil arch of Maya architecture occurs not only in western Pakistan about 400 AD, but also in Islamic *plates 31, 32* and Romanesque architecture. The miniature roofed building inside a temple recurs not only at Ajanta in India, but in Hellenistic architecture and in the ciborium of Christian churches. Sacred tree or cross forms are obviously of Early Christian significance in addition to the late Javanese or Cambodian examples adduced by Ekholm. Court scenes like those of Bonampak or Piedras Negras are common in Byzantine art. Colonnette decorations on facades pertain to Romanesque art as well as to Khmer *plates 33, 34* temples. Corbel-vaulted galleries are Mycenaean as well as Cambodian. Serpent forms, Atlantean figures and phallic statues are *plates 35, 36* not restricted to southeast Asia, but recur throughout the art of the ancient Mediterranean. Doorways framed by monstrous mouths stand in Christian art for the gate to Hell. The Chac Mool figure can be compared to classical rivergods as well as to figures of Brahma. In other words, for nearly every item adduced in this list, an older European parallel can also be proposed. The thesis of Asiatic origins is thus easily diluted to include the entire Old World, and the Asiatic "focus" loses precision.

In addition, these forms all belong to autonomous American iconographic types. The famous comparison between Shang or *plates 37, 38* Chou dynasty bronze scrolls and the scrolls upon Ulua valley vases of about 1000 AD, first pointed out by G. Hentze and revived a generation later by M. Covarrubias, belongs to this class. Chinese bronze scrolls belong to one iconographic series; Ulua valley scrolls pertain to another series. Both series depart from dissimilar sources to converge in an adventitious resemblance that has misled all students who were unaware of the separate typological series embracing each term of the comparison. The argument is like assuming a close blood relationship between persons who look alike, although born many centuries apart, of different races on different continents. The resemblance is accidentally convergent, and it cannot be used to establish a genetic connection without supplementary proofs.

Let us now turn to the modest pretensions of those few historians of art who have treated American antiquity. This modern academic discipline of collecting, selecting, interpreting, and evaluating works of art and architecture owes its origins as a humanistic study to Renaissance historiography (Vasari) and to classical archaeology. Its connections with anthropology have never been close. In the realm of aesthetic choice the history of art treats one-third of all possible human activity. This realm is the main theatre of human volition: it is neither of the senses nor of the intellect, but between them and participating in both.

We have already discussed the anthropologist's restrictive view of the cultural place of artistic activity: let us now look at the art historian's view of the materials of American archaeology. In general, he regards aesthetic products as furnishing symbolic values rather than useful information: he is concerned with intrinsic being more than with applications and derivations.

The task is a difficult one. The term itself, *work of art,* is already a qualitative ranking, as it separates aesthetic products from useful ones. After selecting the works for discussion, we must say how, when, and by whom they were made. Then we must translate their meaning from visual into verbal terms. Finally we have to extract from the historical series of works of art those "durational" meanings that were not apparent to the people themselves who made and used the objects, and which appear only to the historian after the series is completed.

What then is to be our guide in the selection of some objects and the rejection of others? The valuation of whole cultures yields no criterion, for when cultures are ranked, the ranking does not apply to arts: when arts are ranked, the ranking does not apply to cultures. To present knowledge the connection between excellent art and its necessary or adequate social conditions is completely and entirely unexplained. The historian can occasionally point to favoring circumstances, but he cannot identify them as sufficient causes. In short, we know of no type of society in which excellent art inevitably and necessarily appears.

When a building or an object is discussed and illustrated by art historians, it is because of a peculiar perceptual quality. Unlike physical or chemical properties, this perceptual quality cannot be measured. Its presence is unmistakable. It is altogether absent from no artifact. Works of art display it more than utilitarian objects. It is present in nature wherever humans have been active, as in purebred animals, and in selected landscapes. It appears in scenes and things called beautiful as well as in ones that arouse disgust.

It is a special intricacy in several dimensions: technical, symbolic, and individual. In the technical dimension, we are aware with such objects of a long cumulative tradition of stock forms and craft learning, in which the maker's every gesture arises from many generations of experimentation and selection. In the symbolic dimension, we are presented with a cluster of meanings infinitely more complex than the single functional meaning that attaches to a tool or to a bit of information. In the individual or personal dimension we become aware of the maker's sensibility. Through it the technical tradition and the symbolic matter have filtered, undergoing alterations leading to a unique expression.[7]

The net we are using has a mesh that lets the useful forms of material culture pass through it, retaining only those which the field archaeologist calls "fancy" forms. His net, on the other hand, best retains tools and instruments. It lets works of art pass through after only their useful message has been read. Thus we are working over the leavings of the field ethnologists and the archaeologists, like the prospectors who find rare minerals in the tailings of an earlier mine.

If the history of art were merely a matter of solving puzzles of date and authorship, and of explaining works of art, it would be only another antiquarian pursuit among innumerable varieties of gourmandising over the past, along with philately and genealogy. The problem of knowledge itself arises here. The history of art is a historical discipline because the seriation of works of art permits one to transcend the knowledge of the artists themselves about their own work. The modern student of the sculpture of Phidias knows many things about Phidias that neither Phidias nor his contemporaries could know. He who knows the envelope surrounding the events of antiquity, can deduce from this awareness of durational meaning such things as the relative age of any form in a given class of forms, and the significance of an individual artist in a connected series of artists.

In American antiquity many groups of monuments and objects still require seriation, although some anthropological archaeologists have achieved great precision with ceramic stratigraphy and the quantitative analysis of stylistic traits.[8] When it is unlikely that field excavations can solve the problem because the sites are too disturbed, these undifferentiated groups of objects still can be subjected to a stylistic analysis of an art-historical type. Assuming that early and late positions in a series correspond to distinct and definable formal qualities,[9] we can provisionally put *plates 39, 40* the objects in series, as with colossal Olmec stone heads, west *plates 41, 42* Mexican clay sculpture, or Toltec Maya building sequences. These approximations, however coarse and inexact, still are better than no sequence, for it is upon sequence that our awareness of an artistic problem must ultimately rest. The chain of solutions discloses the problem. From many such disclosures we can derive an idea of the guiding configurations of behavior, at different times and places, as experiences corresponding to the aesthetic function in human affairs.

The term "function" needs introduction. In Western thought the concept derives from the Kantian dissection of experience, whence we have the idea of the "pure" artist, the "pure" religious, the "pure" politician, and all the special vocations of the modern age. To be contrasted with such specialized isolates is the relative unity of the functions of the soul elsewhere than in the modern Occident and previous to it:[10] a whole in which religious, ethical, aesthetic, and social functions all were experienced as a seamless entity and conveyed in a single symbolic system of metaphors.

Earlier men could not readily separate the unity of the functions. The men of today cannot bring them back together. We are required to distinguish the functions by the society that has arisen upon their separation. The separation itself permits us to establish an aesthetic function for every experience. Every experience is sensed; it is rationalized; it is laden with emotion. Aesthetic behavior is concerned with emotional states, and it marks the production of every artifact, however simple or useful it may be. Hence an aesthetic function is present in every human product, and by extension, in all cultural behavior.

This extension of an artistic franchise to all artifacts allows a resolution of one great difficulty. In anthropological studies aesthetic value is held to evolve by gradual articulation from the primitive unity of experience along a gradient leading to art as we understand it today. By this evolutionist point of view, aesthetic values are absent from primitive societies. Because all value is regarded as having biological origins, what looks like art in primitive life is believed to have been motivated by utilitarian needs, or by fear, sex, or other "biological drives." Especially favored among social scientists is the theory that art derives from play impulses, and that it serves as a training activity in the struggle for existence.[11]

The opposing point of view is idealist. Here it is a postulate that comprehension of another being is possible only under conditions of similarity between object and subject. Hence we may not restrict the understanding of primitive persons whom we pretend to comprehend, to values only of biological significance, but we must concede them innate values of aesthetic and intellectual bearing essentially akin to our own.[12] Both primitive persons and their modern students share alike in aesthetic behavior. It is a condition of psychic equilibrium between subject and ob-

73

ject. The world is known through emotional states rather than by rational constructs. Natural phenomena are apprehended as states of feeling rather than as events outside consciousness. Unlike the evolutionist, the apriorist apprehends a nucleus of aesthetic value that is the same in all arts: always essential; always definable; always resistant to materialist reductions of its scope. He thus escapes the embarrassment of the evolutionist who, when confronted with early artifacts that look like art, must explain them as non-art.

This conception of the continuum of art can be articulated by the idea of configurations better than by the evolutionist's conception of stages. "Style" rather than "level" is our key to the differences between artistic groupings. Cultural configurations can be charted and measured by the phenomenon of style.[13] Different configurations coexist and succeed one another: each has its own content and its own developmental pattern.

Configurationism, however, is an incomplete and perplexing concept. It is grounded in Gestalt psychology and it transforms the problems into postulates. It elevates the axioms to the rank of explanatory principles.[14] Confronted with the choice between idealist and materialist interpretations, the student of aesthetic behavior must of necessity prefer configurationism to the arbitrary stages of evolutionist thought, for in the latter, aesthetic behavior loses autonomy, and it becomes only the mechanical reflection of other processes.

In conclusion, the domains of scholarship, anthropology and art are not so much in contradiction as complementary to each other, in the relation of studies of content and studies of quality. These apparently rival interests concerned with American antiquity will never starve for want of archaeological materials: the supply seems inexhaustible, and the gradations of quality in each class differ less widely than in the European history of art. One can regret only that nationalistic laws, which regulate the excavation and export of antiquities, actually conduce more to illegal exploitation and to inflationary pricing, than would be the case in a "free trade" situation.

1. The most complete presentation of such schemes is by Gordon Willey and Philip Phillips, *Method and Theory in American Archaeology,* Chicago, 1958.

2. S. G. Morley complained that the native chronicles of Yucatan suffered from "a frequent telescoping of the time scale to make successive events contemporaneous" (*The Ancient Maya,* Stanford 1956, 87). The same tendency appears in the long defense of the Goodman-Martínez-Thompson correlation for Maya dates, by Carnegie Institution of Washington, whose workers thereby joined an ancient tradition on Maya chronology.

3. *Historia general de las cosas de Nueva España,* ed. M. Acosta Saignes, Mexico, 1946, II, 276, 315.

4. Franz Kugler, *Handbuch der Kunstgeschichte,* Stuttgart, 1842, and J. L. Stephens, *Incidents of Travel in Central America,* New York, 1841.

5. I have shown elsewhere, "*On the Colonial Extinction of the Motifs of Precolumbian Art,*" (*Essays honoring S. K. Lothrop,* in press), that utilitarian traits survive or travel more easily than symbolic systems, which are much more perishable. In this context, the diffusionists have yet to explain the translation of Asiatic symbolic forms to America where matters of mere utility failed to "survive".

6. The most complete statement of the new diffusionist arguments is the group of essays entitled *Asia and North America. Transpacific Contacts* (*Memoirs of the Society for American Archaeology*), 9, 1953. For the argument based upon art resemblances, see the essay by Gordon Ekholm, entitled "A Possible Focus of Asiatic Influence in the Late Classic Cultures of Mesoamerica," *ibid.,* 72-89. To be added to his bibliography are the major works by G. Hentze, *Rituals, croyances ... de la Chine antique et de l'Amérique,* Antwerp, 1936; Miguel Covarrubias, *The Eagle, the Jaguar and the Serpent,* New York, 1954; Harold S. Gladwin, *Excavations at Snaketown,* Globe, 1937.

7. On the role of the individual, see the recent essays by R. Trebbi del Trevigiano in *Critica d'Arte,* especially, "Premesse per una storia dell'arte precolombiana," 19 (1957), 22-31.

8. E.g., R. E. Smith, *Ceramics of Uaxactun,* and T. Proskouriakoff, *A Study of Classic Maya Sculpture,* Washington, 1950.

9. This assumption underlies the remarkable stylistic seriation of Nazca pottery by A. Kroeber and A. H. Gayton (UCPAAE, 24, 1927), a seriation recently confirmed by excavations (W. D. Strong, MSAA 13, 1957).

10. E. v. Sydow, *Die Kunst der Naturvölker und der Vorzeit,* Berlin, 1923, 11.

11. A. L. Kroeber, *Antropology,* 1948, 60-1; 390-91.

12. A. Vierkandt, "Prinzipienfragen der ethnologischen Kunstforschung," *Zeitschrift für Ethnologie,* XIX, 1925, 338f.

13. A. L. Kroeber, *Style and Civilizations,* Ithaca, 1957.

14. B. Petermann, *Gestalt Theory,* London, 1932.

PLATES

Plate 1. The rock-shelter of La Colombière, viewed from across the Ain
River

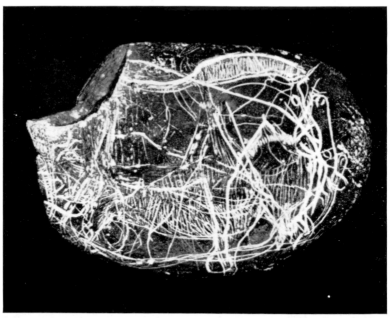

2.1

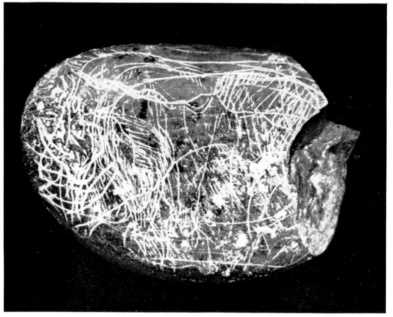

2.2

Plate 3. Rock with "serpentine" engraving found at the Abri Pataud

The La Colombière Pebble
Plate 2.1: obverse surface
Plate 2.2: reverse surface

5

6

Plate 5. Lime container. Geelvink Bay area. Bamboo, 9″ long. Rijksmuseum voor Volkenkunde, Leiden 370-3810

Plate 6. Canoe prow ornament. Geelvink Bay, Biak Island. Wood, fibre, paint, 42½″ high. Leiden 2401-4

Plate 4. The Abri Pataud Venus

7   8

Plate 7. Korwar with human skull. Geelvink Bay, Rumberpon Island, Jembekiri. Wood, 14¼" high. Leiden 2953-1

Plate 8. Korwar. Vogelkop area, Batanta Island. Wood, colored cloth, 19¾" high. Leiden 2432-3

Plate 9. Korwar. Vogelkop area, Waigeu Island. Wood, red and white cotton cloth, 35½" high. Leiden 2432-1

Plate 10. Canoe prow ornament. Humboldt Bay, Tobadi. Wood; brown, black, yellow and white paint; 30" across angle. Leiden 1528-422

9

10

11

12

Plate 13. Tobacco container. Lake
Sentani, Ayafo. Bamboo, 12⅝″
long. Leiden 1528-76   13

Plate 11. Canoe prow. North coast between Jamna Island and Walcke-
naers Bay. Wood, 30⅞″ long. Leiden 1971-1411

Plate 12. Canoe prow ornament. Sarmi area, Masi-Masi Island. Wood,
16¾″ high. Leiden 929-474

Plate 14. Pot. Humboldt Bay, Tobadi. Earthenware; black, yellow and white paint; 9⅞" high. Leiden 1528-37

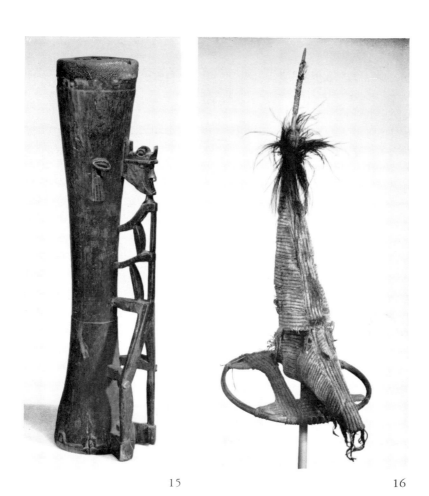

15   16

Plate 15. Drum. Mimika area. Wood, hide, 32¼″ high. Leiden 3375-1

Plate 16. Mask. Mimika area. Rattan; wood; fibre; cassowary feathers; red, black and white paint; length of face 37⅜″. Leiden 1971-997

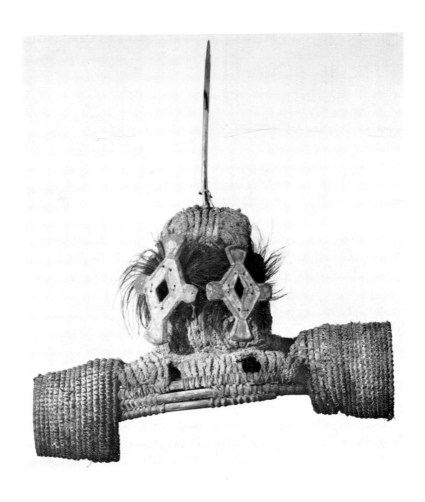

Plate 17. Mask. Mimika area, Koperapoka region, Waonèripi. Rattan, wood, fiber, cassowary feathers; height (omitting stick) 17¾". Leiden 3070-92

18   19

Plate 18. Canoe prow ornament. Mimika area, Utakwa region. Wood, red and white paint, 42⅛″ high. Leiden 1971-527

Plate 19. Female figure. Lorentz River: Asmat. Wood, red and white paint; ear ornaments cassowary feathers and coix lachryma seeds; 31½″ high. Leiden 2412-2

20   21

Plate 20. Food bowl. Lower Eilanden River, Kaimo: Asmat. Wood, red and white paint, 35⅝″ long. Leiden 3070-272

Plate 21. Mask. Kasteel River, Atat: Asmat. Wood, fibre, grass, feathers, seeds, red and white paint. Leiden 3070-212

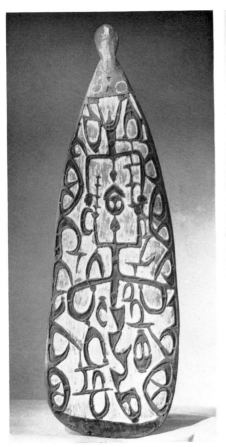

22   23

Plate 22. Shield. Noordoost River: Asmat. Wood; red, white and black paint; 44⅛" high. Leiden 1971-974

Plate 23. Shield. Lower Eilanden River, Warse: Asmat. Wood; fibre; red, white and black paint; 57¼" high. Leiden 3070-254

24   25   26

Plate 24. Shield. Digul River. Wood; fibre; red, white and black paint;
84¼" high. Leiden 2421-1

Plate 25. Shield. Muyu area. Wood; red, white and black paint; 91⅜"
high. Leiden 3452-1

Plate 26. Kui ahat. Marind-Anim. Wood; black, red and white paint;
total height 156¾". Leiden 1447-73

Plate 27. Ugu, the crocodile *dema.* Marind-Anim. Wood; fibre; feathers; red, black and white paint; 39⅜″ high. Leiden 2008-14

28

Plate 28. Drum. Marind-Anim style, collected at Tanas, Jeei area. Wood; white, black, traces of red paint; 36⅝" high. Leiden 3070-472

Plate 29. Lintel 3, Piedras Negras, Guatemala. Maya classic period (first millenium AD); probably a court scene. Stone. Collection University Museum, Philadelphia

Plate 30. Kero. Tiahuanaco, Bolivia. Collected by A. Sawyer. Fine orange clay; orange, black and white slip; 6⅝" high. Collection Mr. and Mrs. Raymond Wielgus, Chicago

29

30

31

32

Plate 32. Shrine in Cave 26, Ajanta, Bombay, India. Courtesy Institute of Fine Arts, New York

Plate 31. Shrine in the Temple of the Cross. Palenque, Chiapas, Mexico. Reconstruction drawing by Tatiana Proskouriakoff. Courtesy Carnegie Institution of Washington

Plate 33. The Palace, Labna, Yucatan, Mexico. Reconstruction drawing
by Tatiana Proskouriakoff. Courtesy Carnegie Institution of Washington

Plate 34. Vieja group. Uxmal, Yucatan, Mexico. Corbel construction, late classic. Courtesy Carnegie Institution of Washington

35

36

Plate 35. Chac Mool. Tula, Hidalgo, Mexico. About AD 1200. Courtesy Mr. John Glass

Plate 36. River God: Nile. Roman, first century AD. Courtesy Institute of Fine Arts, New York

Plate 37. Vase. Ulua Valley, Honduras. Marble, 9⅝" high. AD 1000. Collection University Museum, Philadelphia

Plate 38. Vessel, Kuei. Shang dynasty, 1000 BC. Bronze. Courtesy Institute of Fine Arts, New York

37

38

Plate 39. Head. La Venta, Tabasco, Mexico. Olmec. Stone. Courtesy the National Geographic Magazine,© National Geographic Society

Plate 40. Head. San Lorenzo, Veracruz, Mexico. Olmec. Stone. Courtesy the National Geographic Magazine,© National Geographic Society

Plate 41. Family group. Colima, probably Las Animas. Clay. Middle period. Baltimore Museum of Art, Wurtzburger Collection

Plate 42. Recumbent figure. La Barca, Jalisco; Colima style. Clay. Collection Mr. Diego Rivera